WHAT SHE DOESN'T TELL YOU... BUT YOU SHOULD KNOW

Truths That Transform Men, Relationships, and Lives.

OLIVIA LAMBRAGNO

DEDICATION

To the man who finally chose to look himself in the mirror.
This book is dedicated to you.

Not to the perfect man.
Not to the invincible one.
Not to the man who pretends to be strong.

But to the real man—
the one who makes mistakes, who feels, who stays silent,
who doesn't always know where to begin,
yet keeps moving anyway.

To you, who grew tired of repeating the same patterns.
To you, who decided to stop running.
To you, who realized that strength is not hardness...
it is awareness.

To you, who never had a clear example,
yet are becoming one.
To you, who are facing

wounds you didn't create,
but that you now have the courage to heal.

To you, who chose to read this book
not for entertainment,
but for transformation.

May you find here the courage you didn't know you had,
the clarity you've been missing,
and the certainty that you *can* become
the man you always wanted to be.

This book is yours.
So is this journey.

ACKNOWLEDGMENTS

Some books are written with ideas.
This one was written with stories.

Thank you to the men who—through their successes and their mistakes—gave life to every chapter.
Thank you to those who shared their pain, their confusion, their ego, their fear,
and their sincere desire to do better.

Thank you to the men who dare to read something that confronts them,
yet also supports them.

And thank you to the women:
the ones who love, the ones who wait, the ones who forgive,
the ones who teach without knowing,
the ones who refuse to repeat old patterns,
the ones who inspire men to rise and grow.

And thank you to you, reader, for making it this far,
for not abandoning the process,
for allowing yourself to feel, reflect, recognize, laugh,
be uncomfortable, and heal.

This book exists for one simple reason:
because the world needs better men.
And you are here... starting with yourself.

CONTENTS

Men with dreams but no guidance.
Men who want to grow, change, and become better, but don't know where to begin.

And it was also born **for them**—
for the women who love in silence,
who stay quiet to avoid hurting your pride,
who tolerate more than they should to keep their family together,
who cry in secret because they no longer know how to tell you what they feel…
or because they've told you a thousand times, and still, nothing changes.

And yes, it's also for the other kind of women—
the ones who hurt without reason,
who manipulate,
who don't know how to love,
who stay in a relationship only for convenience, comfort, or status.

In this book, I'm going to speak to you with clarity, with honesty, and without sugarcoating anything.
Not to make you feel guilty,
but to help you see what no one has ever said to you.
To help you understand what a woman feels and thinks, even when she doesn't show it.
To help you see why certain behaviors are keeping you from the life, and the love, you say you want.

Here you will find explanations you were never given:
why you get frustrated so quickly,
why communication feels so hard,
why you repeat the same patterns,
why your fears sabotage you,
why sometimes you destroy what you love,
why you stay where you are not wanted,

why you fear starting over,
and why you remain stuck in relationships that don't fulfill you.

This book is not a criticism.
It is an opportunity.
A guide... at least that is my intention.
A mirror.

And if you choose to read it honestly, not as a perfect man, but as a real one, you will discover something powerful:

Within you lives a stronger, clearer, more grounded, more confident version of yourself.
A version that doesn't betray you.
A version that doesn't hurt others.
A version that *knows how to love.*

That man is waiting for you to wake him up.

Welcome.
Your growth begins here.

PART ONE

A MAN AND HIS INNER WORLD

Identity, self-worth, wounds, habits, and growth.

CHAPTER 1

Self-Worth: When a Man Doesn't Know Who He Is

Truths that transform men, relationships, and lives.

Most men never talk about self-worth. They don't mention it. They don't ask about it. They don't admit they struggle with it.

But many have a **wounded sense of self**—even if they don't realize it.

Because low self-esteem in men rarely appears as sadness. It shows up as **behavior**:

- Aggression
- Jealousy
- Silence
- Exaggerated pride
- Control
- Irresponsibility
- Hurtful jokes
- Tantrums
- Indifference
- That constant "I'm strong, nothing affects me" mask

A man with low self-esteem doesn't cry. He attacks. He hides. He defends. He armors himself.

A man who doesn't know who he is feels the need to prove everything

He must be right.
He must win every argument.
He must feel admired.
He must feel superior.
He must feel needed.
He needs constant validation.

Not because he is strong… but because **deep inside, he feels empty.**

And that emptiness, though painful to acknowledge, is the root of many issues that destroy relationships and lives:

- Failed relationships
- Exhausted women
- Pointless arguments
- Impulsive decisions
- Infidelity
- Uncontrolled jealousy
- Aggression
- Fear of being alone
- Destructive pride

Self-worth is not a "women's issue"

Many men believe self-esteem is only important for women.
But the truth is this:
Self-worth is the foundation of everything in a man's life:

- How he loves
- How he respects himself
- How he works
- How he communicates
- How he responds to pressure
- How he makes decisions
- How he reacts when he feels hurt

A man with healthy self-worth:

- Doesn't need to raise his voice
- Is firm without being violent
- Is confident without arrogance
- Is clear without being hurtful
- Doesn't humiliate or manipulate
- Doesn't control
- Isn't threatened by a woman's independence
- Doesn't compete or compare
- Doesn't boast

A man like this doesn't create fear, he creates peace.

Because a man with healthy self-esteem knows who he is, **with or without applause.** He respects himself. And because he respects himself, he respects others.

A wounded sense of self can destroy what you love

A man who doesn't feel valuable on the inside lives believing that **everything on the outside is a threat.**

That is why this book begins here.

Before we talk about jealousy, communication, infidelity, or relationships... we must talk about **YOU**:

- How you see yourself
- How you speak to yourself
- How much you value yourself
- How you treat yourself

Because here is the truth:

- There is no healthy relationship without a healthy sense of self.
- There is no lasting love with a man who doesn't love himself.
- There is no peace in an insecure heart.

It is **not your fault** that no one taught you this.
But starting today… **it is your responsibility to learn it.**

Your life, your relationship, your character, and your happiness all begin with your **self-worth**.

And this chapter is the first step toward rebuilding it.

CHAPTER 2

Male Insecurity: The Truth No One Ever Told You

Truths that transform men, relationships, and lives.

Male insecurity is a topic almost no one talks about. And even when they do, they rarely explain it clearly. Most conversations lack depth, leaving many questions unanswered.

An insecure man is quickly labeled: "jealous," "possessive," "aggressive," "controlling," "intense," "clingy," or "toxic."

But few people pause to ask: **Where does that behavior come from?**

Because insecurity doesn't appear overnight. It's not a flaw—it's a result.

A silent buildup of old wounds, humiliations, comparisons, abandonment, failures, ridicule, pressure, and unrealistic expectations... that shaped the way a man loves—without him even realizing it.

Where Male Insecurity Is Born

Insecurity is rooted in places most men never dare to examine:

Real Confidence Comes from Within

You have value— with or without a relationship,
with or without applause,
with or without external admiration.

You are not competing with other men.
You are not in danger every time she talks to someone.
You don't need to exaggerate to prove anything.
You don't need to control to feel secure.

You can trust.
You can let go.
You can grow.

Real confidence doesn't come from your body, or your money, or your partner. **Real confidence comes from what you build inside yourself.**

And what you build inside **one can take away.**

Final Message

This chapter isn't here to point fingers.
It's here for you to see yourself.
To recognize yourself.
To tell yourself the truth.

So that one day, you can say with clarity and certainty:

"My security doesn't depend on anyone. It depends on me."

CHAPTER 3

Heal Your Past Before Demanding a Better Future

Truths that transform men, relationships, and lives.

Many men want a healthy relationship… while carrying wounds they never healed.
They want a stable woman… while holding onto unstable emotions.
They want a beautiful future… while staying tied to a broken past.

And that's not how it works.

Because no matter how far you try to move forward,
you will always return to your emotional weak point—until you heal it.

The Weight of Unhealed Wounds

A man doesn't become "difficult" by accident. He becomes difficult because his past left scars he never recognized.

There are silent wounds heavier than any argument:

- a father who abandoned him
- a mother who demanded too much

- childhood comparisons that crushed him
- teenage ridicule that shaped him
- the first woman who betrayed him
- the ex who humiliated him
- the relationship that drained him
- the lie that marked him
- the loss he never overcame
- the mistakes he never forgave himself for

Men rarely talk about these things.
And when they do, they rarely go deep.

But those memories stay alive, hiding and they shape everything:

- his character
- the way he loves
- his patience
- his trust
- his reactions
- his fears
- his frustration
- how he treats a woman
- how he treats himself

Why Healing Cannot Be Outsourced

Let's say it clearly:

No matter how wonderful and supportive the woman beside you is today, healing from past hurts remains essential.

If you don't address and heal what wounded you yesterday, it will resurface tomorrow—no matter how much love surrounds you.

The cycle repeats itself.

Healing is the sole path to ensure that your past does not dictate your future.

What Happens When You Avoid the Past

A man who doesn't deal with his past:

- overreacts
- assumes the worst
- lives defensive
- feels attacked for no reason
- shuts down emotionally
- trusts no one
- suspects everything
- gets frustrated easily
- runs away when he feels real love

Not because he doesn't love,
but because he never learned to love with an open wound.

A woman can love you. She can support you. She can be patient.

But she **cannot** heal what you refuse to face.

Your Past Is Your Responsibility

Your wound is your responsibility.
Your past is your assignment.
Your growth is your path.

Being a man is not about being invincible.
Being a man is having the courage to say:

"This hurt me. This shaped me. And this is what I need to heal."

Healing your past doesn't make you weak, **it makes you free.**

Free from repeating mistakes.
Free from reacting without thinking.
Free from distrust without cause.
Free from sabotaging relationships.
Free from feeling "not enough."
Free from old guilt.
Free from dragging the woman you love into a war she never started.

Final Message

Your future depends on what you resolve today,
not on what your excuses try to hide.

This chapter is an invitation to stop running. To stop covering. To stop pretending.

To tell yourself the truth without fear.

Because a man who heals his past… no longer destroys his present. And finally builds a future worth living.

CHAPTER 4

Fear of Being Alone: Why You Stay Where You Don't Belong

Truths that transform men, relationships, and lives.

Loneliness is a frightening experience, especially for men. Despite what they may say or how they appear, the fear of being alone can be overwhelming. Men might insist, "I'm fine on my own," or even boast about their independence and self-sufficiency. They may project strength, independence, and confidence to those around them.

However, these outward displays often mask the underlying feelings of loneliness and insecurity. The reluctance to admit vulnerability or the need for connection can prevent men from addressing their emotional well-being, further deepening their insecurity.

Deep down, some men carry a quiet fear of being alone with themselves.

And that fear drags them into the worst emotional places: empty relationships. Toxic dynamics. Worn-out marriages. Connections with no love. Homes where respect no longer lives. Stories where they feel trapped. Lives where growth stopped years ago.

Why?

Because for those men, being alone means facing: Their thoughts. Their mistakes. Their emotions. Their guilt. Their emptiness. Their silence. Their lack of identity.

And that terrifies them more than a bad relationship.

That's why so many men:
Stay with someone they no longer love.
Continue relationships that died long ago.
Endure infidelity. Tolerate humiliation.
Maintain marriages for appearance.
Cheat out of fear, not desire.
Lead double lives to avoid making decisions.

Not out of love. Not out of commitment. Not out of responsibility. Out of fear.

Fear of being alone.

And that fear is one of the most expensive things a man can pay.

Because a man who fears solitude: Loses his inner freedom. Loses clarity. Loses dignity. Loses the ability to make mature decisions. Loses the respect of the woman beside him.

A woman can love an insecure, confused, or wounded man… but she cannot admire a man who hides behind fear.

Let me tell you a secret:

Loneliness doesn't destroy you. Staying where you are unhappy does.

There are men who have spent years saying, "I don't want to be here anymore," yet they remain. Not because they love. But because they don't love themselves enough.

The fear of being alone turns a man into a hostage of his own life. It steals his strength. His character. His purpose.

A man who doesn't know how to be alone cannot choose well. He chooses from need, not love. From fear, not wisdom. From comfort, not courage.

Loneliness is not a punishment. It is an opportunity. The space where you grow. Learn. Breathe. Heal. And finally meet yourself.

A man who is comfortable being alone:

Doesn't accept crumbs.
Doesn't tolerate abuse.
Doesn't settle.
Doesn't beg for affection.
Doesn't stay where he is hurt.
Doesn't use lovers as escape routes.
Doesn't betray his values.
Doesn't depend emotionally on anyone.
Chooses with clarity.
Loves with maturity.

Because a man who is whole within himself does not fear losing someone, he knows he never loses himself.

Loneliness isn't your adversary; rather, it's the fear of confronting it that poses the real challenge.

Healing that fear makes you a free man. Free to love. Free to choose. Free to grow. Free to change your life without hesitation.

This chapter is an invitation to discover that you don't need a relationship, a woman, or constant noise to feel valuable. The only thing you truly need is to find yourself.

CHAPTER 5

Fear of Commitment: It's Not Cowardice... It's Confusion

Truths that transform men, relationships, and lives.

When people talk about "fear of commitment," men are often judged harshly. They're labeled cowards, immature, emotionally unavailable, or irresponsible.

But the truth is more complex, and far more human.

Most men don't fear commitment because they don't love.
They fear it because they don't understand it.
They don't fully understand themselves.
They don't understand their emotions.
And no one ever taught them what a healthy, secure relationship truly looks like.

So, commitment doesn't feel like safety.
It feels like stepping into the unknown.

It awakens questions they don't know how to answer:

- What is expected of me?
- What if I fail?

- What if I can't sustain it?
- What if I'm not enough?

Men don't fear the relationship itself.
They fear failing *inside* it.
They fear disappointing.
They fear losing control.
They fear not being capable.
They fear not being "man enough."

This chapter is not about excusing fear.
It's about understanding it—
because what is understood can be healed,
and what is healed can finally be committed.

Commitment is not frightening because of what it is.

It's frightening due to what it brings to the surface.

Commitment brings:
Responsibility.
Consistency.
Loyalty.
Stability.
Patience.
Clarity.
Emotional maturity.

It requires letting go of what's easy
and learning to face problems instead of running from them.
That is intimidating, and with good reason.

Many men grew up believing that commitment is a prison,
a loss of freedom, a surrender of identity.
They were taught that committing means *stopping* life.

Because when a man stops fearing commitment,
he doesn't become trapped.
He becomes powerful.

Choosing.
Staying.
Building.
Caring.
Sustaining.

That is masculinity.

CHAPTER 6

Physical Appearance & Image: What Your Presence Says About You

Truths that transform men, relationships, and lives.

A lot of men believe that "women don't care about a man's looks,"
that "personality is what matters,"
or that "she should love me just the way I am."

And yes, those things are true.
But only to a point.

Because while love is deep, attraction is human.
Admiration is natural.
And neglect… is obvious.

A woman can love a man deeply,
but she cannot admire a man who doesn't take care of himself.

This chapter is not superficial.
It is realistic.

A man's image says far more than whether he looks "good."
It reveals:

- if he respects himself
- if he has discipline
- if he's organized
- if he has energy
- if he lives with purpose
- if he has self-esteem
- if he's responsible
- if he cares about his life
- if he's drowning… or growing

The way you look does not define your worth as a human being—but it *does* reflect the relationship you have with yourself.

Your appearance doesn't make you "better."
But neglect absolutely makes you *less*.

A man who stops taking care of himself sends a clear message:
Nothing matters anymore.
I don't have the energy.
I'm exhausted.
I've given up.
I'm running on autopilot.

And she feels it.

Even if she doesn't say it, it affects her.
Because appearance is not vanity, it's identity.

A cared-for body reflects self-love.
Personal hygiene reflects respect.
Clean clothes show internal order.
A good scent signals consideration.
Grooming shows presence.
A healthy weight reflects emotional and physical well-being.

Respect for yourself.
Respect for your partner.
Respect for the person who shares a bed, a home, a bathroom, a car, and a life with you.

A man who neglects his hygiene isn't just neglecting his body,
he's neglecting his relationship.

Let's talk about the most common hygiene issues in men:

- The famous "quick bath" that doesn't wash anything. Three seconds of water and they think they're clean. That's not bathing—that's wetting the problem.
- Dirty, long, or bitten nails. Few things scream "I don't care about myself" louder than that.
- A dirty or unkempt beard. It doesn't groom itself. It needs to be washed, brushed, and trimmed. And no—just because it's long doesn't mean it's attractive.
- Bad breath. And no, it's not "just because I didn't eat." It's because you didn't brush.
- Clothes that should have been retired years ago. Shirts with holes. Lonely socks. Boxers that are a threat.
- The feet. Let's not even describe that trauma.
- Body odor they believe is "normal." Spoiler: it's not.
- Greasy, unwashed, shapeless hair. Shampoo exists for a reason—and not just as decoration in the shower.

Truth #2

A woman doesn't want perfection. She wants cleanliness.

You don't need to be a model, just be clean.
You don't need expensive cologne—just smell fresh.
You don't need a gym body, just avoid the kind of stomach that screams neglect.

Poor hygiene is not masculinity.
It is abandonment.
And abandonment kills desire.

Truth #3

Hygiene affects everything: intimacy, attraction, and respect.

A man who doesn't take care of himself loses attractiveness. Period.

It affects:

- how she sees you
- how she touches you
- how she connects with you
- how she respects you

Because no woman can admire a man who doesn't even admire himself.

Let me say this again, clearly and from the heart:
Nothing kills desire faster than bad breath.
Especially cigarette breath.
Or a neglected appearance.
Or a body that screams, "I've given up."
Or an odor only *you* think is "normal."

Truth #4

Your body reflects your discipline.

Your scent, your breath, your clothes, your skin, your presence—everything tells a story about you.

Hygiene reveals:

- your order

- your maturity
- your self-esteem
- your self-respect
- your consideration for others

A man who values self-care connects on a deeper emotional level.

Truth #5

If she has to ask you to shower... the relationship is already damaged.

No woman should have to:

- remind you to use deodorant
- ask you to brush your teeth
- beg you to change your clothes
- plead for you to trim your nails
- explain that touching you should feel good

That is not normal.
That is exhausting.
And yes, it kills desire.

Final Message

A man who takes care of his hygiene sends a clear message:
"You deserve the best version of me."

A man who doesn't take care of himself sends the opposite:
"You'll have to settle for the minimum."

You can have a noble heart, good intentions, and a beautiful soul,
but if your presence communicates abandonment,
your relationship will start to crumble long before you notice.

Hygiene is not luxury.
Not vanity.
Not fashion.

Hygiene is coherence.
Hygiene is self-love.
Hygiene is respect.

A man who treasures self-care radiates presence, confidence, and dignity.
And that kind of man?
He's impossible to ignore.

CHAPTER 8

The Male Ego: Your Most Dangerous Enemy

Truths that transform men, relationships, and lives.

The male ego is like a toxic friend that whispers quietly in your ear:

"She's trying to control you."
"Don't let her."
"You're right."
"Don't apologize."
"Don't show feelings."
"Don't change."

It doesn't shout.
It doesn't threaten.
It doesn't hit.

It seduces.

And that is why it is so dangerous.

The ego doesn't destroy relationships with violence.
It destroys them with pride, stubbornness, and a distorted idea of what it means to "be a man."

Many men confuse ego with strength.
They are wrong.

The ego is not confidence.
It is not self-worth.
It is not masculinity.

The male ego is the need to always be right.
The fear of vulnerability.
The inability to apologize.
The obsession with control.
The defensive reaction to any form of criticism.
The terror of being seen as weak.
The constant hunger for validation.
The urge to "win," even if winning costs love.

In simple terms, the ego is the part of a man that loves his image more than it loves his partner.

Inside a relationship, the ego shows itself quietly, but consistently.

A man ruled by his ego struggles to accept mistakes, because being wrong feels like failure.
He becomes defensive easily, turning simple comments into personal attacks.
He competes with the woman beside him, as if the relationship were a battlefield instead of a team.
He needs to control money, decisions, and even the emotional climate of the home.
He avoids apologizing at all costs, choosing silence, distance, or excuses instead of humility.
He confuses authority with superiority and slowly begins to treat his partner as "less."
And when she grows, succeeds, or shines, his ego feels threatened, because her growth reminds him of his own insecurity.

The danger of the ego is not that it makes a man loud.
It's that it convinces him he is right while he is losing everything that matters.

The ego breaks communication.
It creates emotional distance.
It blocks vulnerability.
It destroys trust.
It turns intimacy into tension.
It transforms the home into a silent battlefield.

And the most tragic part?

The ego turns the woman who loves him into the enemy.

Ego and love cannot live in the same home.

Love listens.
The ego defends.

Love grows.
The ego justifies.

Love admits mistakes.
The ego must appear perfect.

Love connects.
The ego divides.

Love requires humility.
The ego survives on pride.

So how does a man defeat his ego?

Not by humiliating himself.
Not by losing his masculinity.
Not by becoming weak.

He defeats it through emotional humility—recognizing that he still has much to learn.
Through self-observation—asking himself whether he is reacting or actually thinking.
Through responsibility—owning mistakes without excuses.
Through listening—not to respond, but to understand.
Through professional guidance, because many egos are fueled by unhealed childhood wounds.
Through consistent inner work, because the ego is stubborn—and growth must be even more persistent.

This chapter holds a truth many men don't want to face:

Some men would rather lose a great woman
than lose an argument.

They end up alone, but "right."

Empty, but victorious in their own mind.

Yet the real victory is something else entirely.

A man who conquers his ego does not become smaller.
He becomes greater.

Greater for himself.
Greater for his life.
Greater for the woman he loves.

CHAPTER 9

Emotional Immaturity: Grown Men with the Emotions of a Child

Truths that transform men, relationships, and lives.

There are men with a beard, a job, a car, responsibilities, and even a family… but emotionally, they never left childhood.

They may be 30, 40, or 50 years old,
but they react like they're seven.

They get offended easily.
They shut down.
They explode.
They avoid serious conversations.
They blame, victimize themselves, disappear, or shout.

Not because they can't do better,
but because they never grew on the inside.

They are adults on the outside,
children on the inside.
And that is something love, patience, or sacrifice cannot fix.

Only maturity can.

She carries the relationship.
She regulates emotions that aren't hers.
She fixes what he avoids.

As she continues to give more and more, he increasingly demands more in return.

A relationship with an immature man drains.
It exhausts.
It confuses.
It wears a woman down in silence.

She begins to feel emotionally tired.
Unsupported.
Alone, even while being with someone.
Guilty for things that are not hers.
Responsible for fixing what he refuses to face.

And the most painful part of all:
she grows... while he stays behind.

Can an emotionally immature man mature?

Yes.
But not because she loves him more.
Not because she waits longer.
Not because she begs.

A man matures when he decides to take responsibility for himself.
When he stops blaming others.
When he seeks help.
When he learns to communicate.
When he faces his childhood wounds instead of running from them.
When he develops self-control, empathy, and emotional awareness.

He doesn't change for love.
He doesn't change out of fear of losing her.
He changes because he wants to become a better man.

Final Message

An emotionally immature man is not evil.
He is simply a child trapped in an adult body.

But a mature man is something else entirely,
an adult with emotional awareness, responsibility, and depth.

And that difference changes everything.

CHAPTER 10

Your Hobbies: Do They Build You — or Slowly Destroy You?

Truths that transform men, relationships, and lives.

A hobby can be a gift.
It can bring peace, balance, joy, and relief.
However, it can also transform into a quiet refuge, one that gradually undermines a relationship without the man even being aware of it.

The problem is not having hobbies.
The problem is **how and why** a man uses them.

Some men use hobbies to recharge.
Others use them to disappear.

And that difference changes everything.

A healthy hobby adds to your life.
It gives you energy instead of stealing it.
It helps you release stress, reconnect with yourself, and return to your relationship more present, more grounded, more alive.

A healthy hobby does not compete with your partner.
It does not replace conversations.

It does not steal essential time.
It does not become an excuse to avoid responsibility.

When a man understands this, he lives better, loves better, and builds better.

But when does a hobby stop being healthy?

A hobby becomes a problem when it turns into avoidance.
When it is used to numb emotions instead of processing them.
When it becomes a substitute for intimacy.
When it is prioritized over the relationship.
When it serves as an escape from conversations, conflict, or emotional responsibility.

At that point, the issue is no longer the hobby itself.
It is what the hobby represents.

Many men say, *"I just need my space,"*
when what they really mean is, *"I don't know how to face what I feel."*

Some hide behind video games that consume hours while their partner becomes emotionally widowed.
Others drown themselves in endless outings, projects, or distractions, always busy, never available.
Some turn alcohol into a "social habit," unaware that it has quietly taken control.
Others spend hours on social media watching other people's lives while neglecting their own.

They stay entertained... but disconnected.

A man can fix cars, bikes, engines, houses—
and still let his relationship fall apart.

Because distraction is not the same as fulfillment.

A hobby that disconnects you from your partner eventually disconnects you from your own life.

CHAPTER 11

"Normal" Addictions: Alcohol, Tobacco & Other Escapes That Destroy More Than You Think

Truths that transform men, relationships, and lives.

There are addictions that don't look like addictions.
"Social" drinking.
The cigarette "to relax."
The daily beer "to take the edge off."
The vape "because everyone uses it."
Gaming.
Gambling.
Porn.
Endless scrolling on social media.

Emotional escape routes.
They are addictions disguised as habits.
As routine.
As "normal."
Accepted by society, encouraged by friends, minimized by men…
but deeply damaging to your life, your identity, and your relationship.

And here is the truth:
Anything you use to avoid feeling, facing, deciding, or changing...
is already an addiction.

Because addiction, in simple terms, is:
the compulsion to repeat a behavior or consume a substance despite its negative consequences.

Alcohol: The cheapest emotional anesthetic

Many men don't drink to celebrate.
They drink to silence themselves.
To stop thinking.
To stop feeling.
To sleep.
To escape loneliness.
To avoid responsibility.
To calm frustration.
To feel "stronger."

But alcohol doesn't relax you. It numbs you.
It doesn't solve anything. It hides everything.
And escapes always send the bill later.

A man who needs alcohol to relax is not relaxed.
He is trapped.
A man who drinks to tolerate his life isn't living.
He is surviving.

Alcohol doesn't destroy instantly.
It slowly destroys:

- respect
- presence
- energy

- character
- relationships
- dignity

A woman can sense when the man next to her is no longer himself, but rather a numb version of who he truly is.

Tobacco: An emotional contradiction

Men say:
"It's just a cigarette."
"It calms me."
"It's my moment."

But cigarettes, cigars, or vape devices:
don't calm, don't help, don't resolve anything

They simply steal years from your life,
and life from your years.

Men may believe they "control the habit," but the truth is:
the habit controls them
anxiety fuels their actions
their body bears the consequences
their partner endures the strain

The problem isn't the tobacco itself.
It's what the tobacco hides:

- anxiety
- unmanaged stress
- emotional voids
- ignored wounds
- unprocessed emotions

Modern escapes: Porn, gaming, social media & gambling

Here comes an uncomfortable truth:
Most men don't watch porn for pleasure,
they watch it to avoid real emotional intimacy.

Many don't play video games for fun,
they play to avoid facing their life.

Others don't live on social media as a hobby,
they live there because their reality feels heavy.

And countless men don't gamble for the adrenaline,
they gamble to feel control over something in their life.

These are emotional escapes.
Temporary patches.
Distractions that numb but never heal.
Every escape reveals a pain they refuse to face.

Why do men fall into "normal" addictions?

They don't know how to manage emotions
No one taught them to talk, cry, ask for help, or express frustration.

They feel constant pressure
Provider, stable, strong, perfect. Escape becomes the only "release."

They choose what's immediate
Quick reward is easier than slow progress.

They haven't healed their wounds
Every addiction is a symptom, not the real problem.

They believe they're not hurting anyone
The most dangerous self-deception.

The real damage (what you don't see... but she does)

A man who seeks refuge in escape:

- isn't present
- doesn't build
- doesn't grow
- doesn't connect
- doesn't move forward

And the woman beside him begins to feel:

- emotionally abandoned
- disconnected
- distanced
- frustrated
- lonely
- exhausted
- disappointed
- undesired
- deeply worn out

Because she wants a **partner**
not an emotional child.
Not a quiet addict.
Not a man who disappears into screens, bottles, smoke, or fantasies.

The transformational truth

Addiction doesn't define you.
What defines you is your willingness to face it.

A grown man recognizes when something controls him
and decides to reclaim his life.

Not out of fear.
Not out of shame.
Out of dignity.

A strong man asks for help.
A mature man sets limits.
A conscious man protects his health.
A responsible man guards his energy.
A wise man chooses his future.

You don't have to cease living,
you simply need to stop hiding.

The life you desire lies just beyond the escape that currently holds you back.

CHAPTER 12

Aggression & Emotional Violence: When Your Anger Says More About You Than Your Words

Truths that transform men, relationships, and lives.

Some men believe violence only means hitting.
That aggression is only yelling.
That abuse is only humiliation.

But emotional violence is often silent.
It doesn't leave bruises—
it leaves **scars no one sees**.

What Emotional Aggression Looks Like

Aggressive men don't always raise their voices.
Sometimes, aggression sounds like silence.
Or looks like control.
Or hides behind sarcasm and indifference.

It can show up as:

- frustrated sighs
- cutting replies
- ignoring
- ridiculing
- speaking with superiority
- minimizing problems
- invalidating emotions
- slamming doors
- silent treatment
- making her feel dumb
- blaming her for everything

Emotional aggression corrodes relationships.
It doesn't manifest in a single outburst, instead,
it seeps in gradually, eventually leading to the death of connection.

Why Do Men Become Aggressive?

They never learned to express emotions
Anger becomes the mask for sadness, fear, or exhaustion.

They carry unhealed wounds
Childhood pain, rejection, abandonment, or trauma becomes a shield.

They're insecure
Yes, aggression often hides low self-worth.
The louder the man, the lower his inner confidence.

They confuse control with respect
They think leading is imposing. That being feared means being respected.

They grew up with aggression
What's normalized in childhood becomes repeated in adulthood.

They're afraid
Of losing, of being vulnerable, of being exposed.
So they attack before anyone gets too close.

The Truth Many Avoid

Aggression is not power.
It's **a loss of emotional control**.

A man who explodes isn't showing strength,
he's revealing instability.

Real strength is:

- thinking before speaking
- feeling without wounding
- breathing before reacting
- calming yourself without being asked
- seeking help instead of causing harm

What Aggression Does to a Relationship

It:

- kills desire
- destroys admiration
- breaks trust
- creates fear
- increases distance
- damages her mental health
- forces her to live in caution
- steals her self-worth
- replaces love with survival

Women don't fall in love with aggression.
They adapt to survive it—until they finally leave.
And once they're gone, they realize how much they tolerated... just to keep the peace.

Can an Aggressive Man Change?

Yes.
But not with promises.
Not with silence.
Not with gifts, flowers, apologies, or sex.

Real change begins with:

- self-awareness
- humility
- emotional education
- therapy
- daily self-discipline
- consistency
- accepting full responsibility

Changing isn't saying "I'll do better."
It's becoming someone better.

Final Message

An aggressive man is not strong.
True strength is emotional maturity,
the ability to master yourself, not others.

You are not respected because you intimidate.
You are respected when you protect.
You are loved when your presence brings peace, **not fear.**

Emotional Roots of Intimacy Struggles

Stress floods the body with cortisol and blocks pleasure.
Performance anxiety turns closeness into pressure.
Unspoken conflict creates emotional distance.
Resentment erodes connection.
Self-rejection creates fear of being rejected.
Porn use can desensitize and distort expectations.
Guilt or trauma can shut the body down as self-protection.

What She Feels—Even If She Doesn't Say It

When intimacy fades, she starts to question herself.
"Am I still attractive to him?"
"Did I do something wrong?"
"Is there someone else?"
"Does he still love me?"

She may not say it out loud, but she feels it.

Few things affect a woman more deeply than feeling unwanted.

How a Man Begins to Heal

Healing starts with **honesty**.
Naming the emotions removes the weight of silence.
Talking openly reduces pressure.
Understanding the cause brings clarity.

Intimacy is not a test.
It's not performance.
It's **connection**.

Improving emotional well-being, caring for mental and physical health, restoring affection and presence—these rebuild trust in the body.
And when a man reconnects with himself, he can reconnect with her.

Final Truth

A man who is unwell within himself cannot be fully present with his partner.
The body is not failing him.
It's telling the truth he's been avoiding.

When a man chooses to face it,
intimacy becomes what it was meant to be again,
not pressure, not silence, not distance, but real connection.

CHAPTER 14

Boring Men: Emotionally Dead, Routine-Driven, and Without Spark

Truths that transform men, relationships, and lives.

This is one of the most uncomfortable truths:
A man doesn't need to be abusive or unfaithful to destroy a relationship.
He only needs to be emotionally absent.

There are good men.
Responsible men.
Hard-working men.
But also, disconnected men.

Men who checked out emotionally years ago.
They don't initiate.
They don't feel.
They don't grow.
They don't change.

They are present… but lifeless.
Like furniture: useful, silent, still.
They don't hurt anyone.
But they slowly kill the energy of the relationship.

Living with a man who has no inner world
is like living with a ghost.
He's there, but he isn't.

What Is a Boring Man?

A boring man:

- proposes nothing new
- lives tired
- has no passions or dreams
- doesn't grow
- doesn't initiate change
- repeats the same routine endlessly
- spends hours numbing himself with screens
- lacks direction, purpose, or fire
- believes "this is just how I am" is enough

But it isn't.

A woman doesn't want perfection.
She wants to feel **alive** beside him—
not emotionally aged by his presence.

What a Boring Man Causes in a Relationship

- **Kills desire**
  She can desire an imperfect man, but not an inert one.
- **Drains her feminine energy**
  She becomes cold or distant, not from lack of love,
  but because nothing in him moves.
- **Creates silent distance**
  Conversation, complicity, and dreams fade.

- **Destroys admiration**
  Admiration is not about success.
  It's about **vision, creativity, inner drive**.
- **Disconnects intimacy**
  Without emotional movement, physical connection becomes routine—not passion.

Why So Many Men Become This Way

1. **They live on autopilot**
   Each day repeats the last.
2. **They've lost their purpose**
   Without purpose, there's no spark.
3. **They fear change**
   Not laziness, fear.
4. **They confuse stability with stagnation**
   They stop evolving.
5. **They only learned to work, never to live**
   Pleasure and play feel foreign.
6. **They have no inner world**
   No goals. No curiosity. No fire.
7. **They've become conformists**
   "I'm not complaining."
   But the relationship is.

What He Doesn't See (But She Feels Deeply)

A woman doesn't get bored overnight.
First, she tries:

- to inspire him
- to involve him
- to ignite something

- to dream beside him

Until she realizes the truth:
It's not that he can't—he simply won't.

And that's when she stops trying.
That's when the bond begins to die.

Boredom doesn't explode.
It **withers**.
It's the silent death of connection.
It leaves no chaos—just emptiness.

A woman doesn't leave because she stopped loving.
She leaves because she stopped **living** beside him.

Final Message

This chapter isn't an accusation.
It's a call to **wake up**.

If you see yourself in this move.
Feel again.
Dream again.
Act.
Initiate.
Create.

Because the man who comes back to life doesn't just rebuild the relationship—**he rebuilds himself.**

PART TWO

THE MAN AND HIS RELATIONSHIPS

Emotions, communication, love, family, fidelity, and connection.

CHAPTER 15

Why Some Men Can't Maintain a Relationship

Truths that transform men, relationships, and lives.

Countless men say they want a stable, healthy, beautiful relationship, but in practice, they can't sustain it.

They start strong: attentive, present, affectionate, excited.

And then, without bad intentions but driven by unconscious behavior, they begin to destroy what they themselves built

It's not bad luck.

It's not "women are too complicated."

It's not fate.

There are profound emotional, psychological, and behavioral factors that contribute to why a man may lose what he claims to desire. Until he confronts these issues, he will find himself trapped in the same narrative—over and over again.

5. They fear vulnerability

Opening, crying, sharing, admitting mistakes… for them, this equals weakness.

But here's the truth:

A man who doesn't let himself be seen can't be truly loved.

Vulnerability doesn't take strength away, it removes the armor that stops connection.

6. They have not yet resolved their past

Trauma, abandonment, infidelity, emotional neglect, rejection, humiliation, childhood wounds…

What you don't heal, you repeat.
What you don't face controls you.
What you don't resolve, sabotages you.

A new relationship cannot carry the ruins of the past.

7. They have unrealistic expectations

They want:

a perfect woman
love without effort
a relationship without conflict
intimacy without emotional connection
support without providing support
a partner without commitment

Idealized love destroys real love.

8. They confuse interest with control

When she asks for communication, they hear control.
When she asks for clarity, they feel pressured.
When she asks for attention, they feel limited.
When she asks for commitment, they believe she wants to change them.

They can't tell the difference between a healthy boundary
and imagined control.

And that confusion slowly destroys what they should be protecting the most.

9. They live from deep insecurity

An insecure man is constantly at war with himself.

He compares himself.
He feels insufficient.
He competes with his partner instead of growing beside her.
He gets offended easily.
He misinterprets words and intentions.
He depends on constant validation to feel worthy.

No relationship can survive
when one person is at war with himself every single day.

10. They don't know how to be a partner—only an individual

Being a partner is not about losing yourself.
It is about learning how to build something shared.

It requires negotiation.
Empathy.

Compromise.
Listening.
Shared priorities.
Teamwork.

Some men never learn how to create a *"we."*
They live from *"me, me, me."*

And ego eventually destroys what love tries to build.

11. They get bored when everything is fine

Some men become addicted to drama, chaos, conflict,
or the adrenaline of the chase.

When a relationship becomes stable, mature, and safe,
they don't feel peace, they feel empty.

Why?

Because they never learned how to live without emotional noise.

Where there is no inner peace, outer stability feels boring.

12. They don't understand consistency

They are intense at the beginning and distant later.

Passionate at first, absent with time.

They confuse infatuation with love.
Emotion with commitment.

But real love doesn't end when emotion fades,
it begins when decision appears.

Final Note

A man does not lose a woman because she stops loving him.

He loses her because his fears, habits, and lack of growth
don't allow him to sustain what his heart says it wants, but his maturity cannot hold.

CHAPTER 16

How to Choose Your Partner (and What Not to Choose)

Truths that transform men, relationships, and lives

Choosing a partner is not a game.
Yet many men make decisions as if it were one, and that is why they repeatedly end up in relationships that drain them, confuse them, or slowly wear them down.

Later, they ask themselves:
"Why does this always happen to me?"

The answer is uncomfortable, but necessary:

It's not fate.
It's choice.

The partner you choose shapes your peace, your growth, your emotional stability, your decisions, and ultimately, your future.

Before repeating the same stories, it's important to gain some clarity.

Don't Choose from Emptiness

Some men look for a partner to fill what they haven't faced within themselves.

Loneliness.
Insecurity.
The need for attention.
The need for validation.
The desire to feel important.
Emotional dependency.

When you choose a partner from a place of pain, you don't choose someone who will help you heal. Instead, you tend to choose someone who feeds that same wound.

If you are not well with yourself, you don't choose a partner.
You choose relief.

And relief never builds a healthy relationship.

Don't Choose Only from Desire

Yes, chemistry matters.
Yes, attraction matters.

But when a man chooses only with his body, he often ends up sharing life with someone who fits him in bed, but not in real life.

The bedroom does not sustain a relationship.
Respect does.
Communication does.
Shared values do.
Emotional stability does.

Chemistry ignites the spark.
Compatibility keeps the fire alive.

Choose Emotional Maturity

Emotional maturity is not perfection.
It is responsibility.

A mature woman does not manipulate to feel secure.
She does not punish with silence.
She does not create drama to feel seen.
She expresses herself without destroying.
She listens without attacking.
She takes responsibility for her actions.
She understands that a relationship is built by two.

Just as an emotionally immature man can wreak havoc on a woman's life, and an emotionally immature woman can profoundly impact a man's life as well.

Maturity protects.
Immaturity drains.

Choose a Woman Who Respects Herself

A woman who lacks self-respect will find it difficult to honor boundaries, value the relationship, and maintain her own peace—much less yours.

A woman who values herself does not accept crumbs.

And she will not offer them either.

Self-respect sets the standard for how love is lived.

Choose Values, Not Excuses

Values are not negotiable.

Honesty.
Responsibility.

Loyalty.
Emotional stability.
Ethics.
Life vision.
Respect.

When a man chooses based on values, he chooses a future.
When he chooses based on impulses, he chooses problems.

Attraction fades.
Character remains.

What You Should Never Choose

Without filters or excuses:

Do not choose aggression disguised as passion.
Do not choose manipulation disguised as vulnerability.
Do not choose disrespect disguised as honesty.
Do not choose toxic jealousy disguised as love.
Do not choose someone who refuses to work on herself.
Do not choose someone who never takes responsibility.
Do not choose emotional punishment.
Do not choose stagnation.

Many men choose quickly and regret slowly.

Before Choosing Her, Choose Yourself

Here is the core truth of this chapter:

A man who does not know himself
will repeatedly choose the wrong partner.

A man who knows who he is chooses with clarity.

Before choosing a woman, work on yourself.
Heal your past.
Build your self-worth.
Define your goals.
Strengthen your identity.
Clarify your purpose.

When you are well with yourself,
you choose from fullness, not from lack.

A whole man chooses a whole woman.

That is not a slogan.
It is the result of inner work.

The right partner is not found.
She is chosen.

And only a growing man can choose
with a clear mind and an awakened heart.

CHAPTER 17

Jealousy: When Your Fear Destroys What You Love

Truths that transform men, relationships, and lives.

Jealousy is not love.
It is not protection.
It is not care.
It is not interest.

Jealousy is fear.

Fear of losing.
Fear of not being enough.
Fear that someone else will take your place.
Fear of repeating an old, painful story.
Fear of having your insecurity exposed.

And when that fear is not recognized or worked through, it becomes one of the fastest ways to destroy the very thing you claim to love.

Jealousy Says More About You Than It Does About Her

A faithful, emotionally mature woman does not deserve to pay for wounds she did not create.

Jealousy rarely has to do with what she does.
It has everything to do with what you feel.

Low self-worth.
Insecurity.
Fear of abandonment.
Unhealed emotional wounds.
Past experiences of betrayal.
The need for control.
Comparison with other men.

Jealousy does not say, *"I love her."*
Jealousy says, *"I don't trust myself."*

Jealousy Turns You into the Enemy of Your Own Relationship

A jealous man slowly becomes someone he never intended to be.

He monitors.
He questions.
He demands explanations.
He interprets everything as a threat.
He restricts.
He checks.
He accuses.

And in the process, he suffocates the relationship.

Not because love is missing, but because peace is.

Women rarely leave because they stop loving.
They leave because they are emotionally exhausted.

Jealousy Distorts Who You Are

Insecurity reshapes a man into a version of himself he barely recognizes.

He becomes impulsive instead of calm.
Controlling instead of protective.
Anxious instead of confident.
Reactive instead of grounded.

Jealousy changes tone, energy, reactions, and presence.
And it destroys something that is not easily rebuilt:
dignity.

Jealousy Exposes Your Inner Voids

When a man does not know who he is,
he tries to control what she does to feel safe.

When he does not value himself,
he looks for constant proof that she values him.

When he does not trust himself,
he demands evidence that she is faithful.

But a relationship cannot carry the weight of unresolved wounds.
Those wounds are yours to heal,
not hers to manage.

When Jealousy Goes Unchecked, It Escalates

At first, jealousy whispers.

Questions that sound harmless.
Doubts disguised as concern.
Curiosity masked as care.

But when fear is left untreated, it grows.

What began as insecurity turns into control.
What looked like love becomes surveillance.
What sounded like worry turns into punishment.

A jealous man often says, *"I'm not like this."*
And yet, he is because he is not addressing what he created.

Jealousy Can Be Healed—But Only with Courage

Not with force.
Not with pride.
Not with shouting.
Not with excuses.

Jealousy heals when a man is willing to look inward.

When he acknowledges the problem instead of denying it.
When he seeks support if needed.
When he builds real self-worth.
When he heals past wounds.
When he expresses fear without attacking.
When he learns to trust.
When he releases the need to control.

The woman you love is not your property.
She is your partner.

The Painful Truth That Liberates

Your jealousy does not protect the relationship.
It damages it.

And often, it creates exactly what you fear the most:
distance.

No woman wants to spend her life proving her innocence.
No woman wants to feel monitored.
No woman wants to be treated like a suspect without cause.

Loving means trusting.
And trusting is emotional maturity.

Healthy love feels like freedom, not a prison.
Like calm, not tension.
Like partnership, not surveillance.

If you want to stop destroying what you love,
work on yourself.

Look inward.
Identify your wounds.
Heal what still hurts.
Learn to trust.
Stop confusing control with love.

It isn't love.
It never was.

CHAPTER 18

Possessive Men: When Control Is Mistaken for Love

Truths that transform men, relationships, and lives

Some men are not looking for a partner.
They are looking for possession.

They want a woman who revolves around them,
who adapts to their world,
who limits herself so they can feel secure.

They call it *care.*
They call it *protection.*
They call it *love.*

But it is not love.
It is control.

And the most dangerous part is this:
many men don't even realize they are doing it.

They think they are "establishing boundaries," but in truth, they are stifling the relationship.

A Man Is Not Born Possessive—He Becomes One

No man wakes up one day wanting to control another human being.

Possessiveness is built over time, shaped by insecurity, fear of abandonment, emotional wounds, family patterns, and a fragile sense of self-worth.

It often grows in men who never developed a solid identity,
who confuse love with surveillance,
and who believe control is the only way to feel safe.

The truth is simple, even if it's uncomfortable:

A possessive man does not protect what he loves.
He imprisons what he is afraid of losing.

How Possessiveness Begins

It rarely starts with aggression.

It starts quietly, disguised as concern.
As comments that seem harmless.
As questions that sound reasonable.

At first, it feels like attention.
Then it becomes monitoring.
Then restriction.
Then interrogation.

What once felt like being accompanied
slowly turns into being watched.

And that is the moment when a woman stops feeling safe
and starts feeling trapped.

Final Message

This chapter is not intended to bring you shame. Instead, it aims to awaken your awareness.

To help you recognize where possessiveness comes from,
what feeds it, and how to stop repeating it.

It is an invitation to leave behind the man who suffocates
and become the man who brings peace.

Because love does not cage.
Love does not monitor.
Love does not restrict.

Love chooses.
And it allows choice in return.

CHAPTER 19

When She No Longer Desires You: What It Really Means

Truths that transform men, relationships, and lives.

There is a truth many men still don't want to accept:
when a woman stops desiring you, it is not out of caprice, punishment, or lack of love.

The loss of female desire is a message.
A symptom.
An emotional alarm.
A silent cry that says, *"Something between us broke."*

But because most men only see the result—her coldness—they fail to see the emotional path that led her there.
I hope today you can understand it.

Female desire is emotional before it is physical

A man can feel desire even when he is tired or upset.
A woman usually cannot.

The female body responds directly to how she feels inside:

- how she is looked at
- how she is listened to
- how she is valued
- how she is respected
- how she is treated in daily life
- how safe she feels
- how emotionally accompanied she feels
- how she is spoken to
- how she cared for

If she does not feel emotionally connected, her body shuts down.
That simple. That deep.

A woman doesn't lose desire—she loses the bond

Female desire is born from emotional connection.

When a relationship fills with tension, indifference, or pain, desire simply has no place to exist.

Many men conclude:
"She doesn't love me anymore."
"There must be someone else."
"She just got cold for no reason."
"I'm not attractive to her anymore."

But no, my dear.
What faded was the emotional connection.
And where there is no connection, desire cannot survive.

A woman's coldness reflects a man who stopped connecting

A woman grows cold when she:

- stops feeling loved
- stops feeling seen
- stops feeling chosen
- stops feeling valued
- stops feeling respected
- stops feeling safe
- stops feeling important

If for months she sent signals you didn't see, or didn't want to see, don't expect her body to respond as if nothing happened.

A woman's body does not lie.
When it shuts down, it's because something hurt her.

Men often look for the solution in the wrong place

When she no longer desires them, many men:

- get angry
- pressure her
- complain
- demand
- grow frustrated
- blame her
- feel "less of a man"
- pull away
- look for another woman
- give up

And all that shuts her down even more.

Why?
Because she doesn't need pressure.
She needs connection.

Restoring desire does NOT begin in the bedroom

This is another truth most men don't know:
female desire begins in the mind and the heart, not in the body.

If you want to restore her desire:

- speak to her with tenderness again
- look at her with attention again
- treat her with respect again
- truly listen to her again
- be her partner again
- flirt with her again
- make her feel safe again
- surprise her again
- see her as a woman, not as routine
- choose her again

Desire returns when connection returns.

True masculinity repairs—it does not pressure

A mature man:

- asks
- observes
- reflects
- takes responsibility
- acknowledges his faults
- commits

- works on himself
- rebuilds the connection
- and courts her again like the first time

Because desire fading is not an ending.
It is a warning.
An opportunity to grow.

The final truth

When a woman stops desiring you, you don't lose sex.
You lose something far greater:

The emotional bridge that makes a relationship alive, real, and deep.

And if you have the humility to understand it
and the courage to work on it,
you can not only restore her desire…

You can restore something even more valuable: her heart.

CHAPTER 20

Infidelity: The Truth Most Men Refuse to Admit

Truths that transform men, relationships, and lives

Numerous men believe infidelity is "something that happens."
That "everyone does it."
That "it's part of being a man."
Or that "it was just a mistake, it meant nothing."

However, the reality, one that many men frequently avoid confronting, is this:

Infidelity does not begin in the bed.
It begins long before that.

It begins in the mind.
In the ego.
In insecurity.
In disrespect.
In small decisions that slowly become normal.

Infidelity is not an accident.
It is a series of conscious choices made long before the final act.

Here's a truth that many men may find difficult to accept:

Infidelity says nothing about the woman.
It says everything about the man.

It speaks of emptiness.
Of emotional immaturity.
Of the need for validation.
Of the inability to face problems directly.
Of avoiding responsibility.

A man who respects himself does not need betrayal to feel alive.
And a man who respects his partner does not use another woman's body to feed his ego.

Why Men Cheat

Infidelity often grows from a fragile ego.

For some men, cheating becomes a way to reassure themselves:
"I'm still desirable."
"I still matter."
"I still have power."

It is a temporary relief for much deeper insecurity.

For others, infidelity is an escape.

When the relationship enters difficult moments, they do not communicate, repair, or grow.
They avoid discomfort.
They avoid accountability.
They seek silence through distraction and gratification.

Some confuse desire with love.
They mistake excitement for connection,

and attraction for intimacy,
never learning that real love requires presence, not impulse.

Many never learned fidelity at all.

They grew up hearing that cheating is normal, expected, or even celebrated as long as no one finds out.
They continue operating from outdated, primitive beliefs without questioning them.

And then there are those who cheat simply because they want to.

Not because of wounds.
Not because of trauma.
Not because of emotional emptiness.

They cheat because they enjoy the game.
Because it feeds their ego.
Because they believe multiple women increase their value.
Because they confuse promiscuity with masculinity.

Repeated, justified infidelity is not a mistake.
It is a pattern.
A lifestyle.
A chronic emotional immaturity.

And the most tragic part is this:

A man who boasts about cheating does not show power.
He reveals emptiness.
A fragile identity.
A lack of evolution.

And without realizing it, he does not only destroy relationships,
he damages women, families, and himself.

The Truth They Don't Want to Hear

Infidelity always leaves scars.

Trust, once broken, never returns in the same form.
She may forgive, but she will never forget.
And the man who betrays never comes back unchanged either.

"It was only once" is not an explanation.
It is an excuse.

The real question is not, *"Why did you cheat?"*
The real question is:
"What were you avoiding facing within yourself?"

Infidelity does not make you a man.
It does not make you strong.
It does not make you desired.
It does not make you free.

It makes you poor—
poor in character,
poor in discipline,
poor in emotional control,
poor in integrity.

A faithful man is not faithful because he lacks options.
He is faithful because he chooses his values, his word, and his partner every single day.

Real Stories Men Rarely Tell

While writing this chapter, I spoke with men who shared real experiences—stories that confirm everything above.

CHAPTER 21

The Good Man Who Forgot Himself

When kindness turns into self-abandonment

There are men who are not aggressive.
Not unfaithful.
Not violent.
Not cruel.

They are good men.

Too good.

Men who give.
Who forgive.
Who tolerate.
Who stay quiet.
Who adapt.
Who sacrifice themselves repeatedly in the name of love.

And little by little, they disappear.

When Being "Good" Becomes Self-Abandonment

Some men confuse love with endurance.
They believe loving means giving up everything, enduring everything, always believing.

They learned, often very early, that their needs matter less.
That saying "no" makes them selfish.
That setting boundaries risks abandonment.
That being loved requires pleasing.

So, they stay.
Even when it hurts.
Even when they are humiliated.
Even when they are emotionally mistreated.

Not because they are weak.
But because they are afraid of being alone.

The Man Who Attracts Women Who Take Too Much

There are women who sense this type of man immediately.
A man full of empathy.
Of guilt.
Of responsibility.
Of fear of conflict.

And some of them, consciously or not, take advantage of it.

They control.
They manipulate.
They punish.
They demand.
They threaten with abandonment.
They erode their self-esteem little by little.

This is not love.
This is emotional exploitation.

And it can be just as destructive as any other form of abuse.

Why Does a Man Allow This?

Because deep down, he does not believe he deserves better.

Because he learned that love is something you earn by suffering.
Because he mistakes loyalty for self-erasure.
Because his self-worth depends on being needed.
Because the idea of starting over feels more terrifying than staying miserable.

And sometimes, because he believes this is the best he will ever get.

Kindness Without Boundaries Is Not Love

Being a good man does not mean tolerating disrespect.
Being loving does not mean accepting abuse.
Being loyal does not mean betraying yourself.

Love should not require you to shrink.
Or disappear.
Or lose your voice.

A relationship that only works when you stay silent is not a relationship.
It is a cage.

The Invisible Sadness of These Men

These men often carry a quiet, dignified sadness.

They don't complain.
They don't scream.
They don't play the victim.

They simply grow tired.
Older.
Lonelier, sometimes even while married.

And many of them repeat the same pattern, wondering why they always attract the same kind of woman.

The answer is painful but liberating:

You don't attract what you want.
You attract what you believe you deserve.

Learning to Choose Yourself

Healing for these men begins with one terrifying realization:

Loving yourself is not selfish.
Leaving what hurts is not failure.
Being alone is not worse than being destroyed slowly.

A good man does not become less loving when he sets boundaries.
He becomes healthier.

When he learns to say "no,"
to protect his peace,
to value his dignity,
to walk away from emotional abuse,
to choose himself, he doesn't lose love.

He finally becomes capable of real love.

It doesn't.

Communication is the ability to understand what your partner feels, thinks, and needs, even when it makes you uncomfortable.

It requires something many men were never taught:
leaving the ego outside the conversation.

A man who learns to truly listen gains something invaluable:
emotional mastery.

Talking Without Fighting Begins with Not Reacting

When a woman says something uncomfortable, many men react immediately.
They defend themselves, raise their voice, minimize her feelings, attack, change the subject, or walk away.

And at that exact moment, communication dies.

The conversation stops being about understanding
and turns into conflict.

The rule is simple, but powerful:

Pause.
Breathe.
Listen.

Respond, don't react.

Running Away Is Not Calm—It Feels Like Abandonment

One of the most common masculine habits is emotional escape.

When she wants to talk, he postpones.
He distracts himself.
He goes silent.
He shuts down.

From his perspective, he avoids conflict.
From hers, he disappears.

What you avoid today becomes tomorrow's emotional explosion.

Avoidance does not protect the relationship.
It slowly erodes it.

How to Speak Without Creating a War

Healthy communication does not accuse.

When a man speaks from blame, the body tenses and the heart closes.
When he speaks from experience, the conversation opens.

Instead of attacking with absolutes, he expresses what he feels and perceives.
This lowers defenses and invites dialogue.

Listening, truly listening, is not staying silent while preparing a response.
It is presence.

It is eye contact.
It is patience.
It is allowing her to finish.
It is making sure you understand before responding.

Sometimes, the most powerful phrases are not explanations, but acknowledgments:

"I understand now."
"That makes sense."
"Thank you for telling me."

No argument wins what understanding achieves.

Regulating Your Emotions Is Masculine Strength

Most men do not fight because of what she says.
They fight because they do not know how to manage what they feel.

Feeling attacked, insecure, frustrated, or uncomfortable is not weakness.
Not knowing how to express it is.

Maturity is not silence.
And it is not aggression.

Maturity is the ability to say what you feel without destroying the other person.

Words Can Heal—or Harm

Some men use communication as a weapon.
They punish with silence, cut with sarcasm, manipulate with words, bring up old wounds, or shut conversations down abruptly.

That is not communication.
That is emotional violence.

Respect is not optional.
It is the foundation.

Talk to Unite, Not to Win

The real question in a conflict is never *"Who is right?"*
The real question is *"How do we solve this without hurting each other?"*

Healthy communication seeks connection, clarity, understanding, and growth.
Never domination.

When a woman feels heard, something changes.
Her defenses lower.
Her trust deepens.
Her openness grows.
Peace returns.
Desire follows.

Communication does not transform a relationship overnight,
but it transforms it permanently.

The Final Truth

Many men do not lose the woman they love because love disappears.
They lose her because communication never existed.

A woman can endure many struggles.
But she cannot endure feeling invisible, invalidated, or unheard.

Learning to communicate is not a luxury.
It is an emotional necessity.

And without question,
it is one of the clearest signs of true masculinity.

CHAPTER 23

Why a Man Stays in a Relationship That No Longer Works

Truths that transform men, relationships, and lives.

Some relationships end… but stay alive.
Bodies present, souls absent.
Routine, not affection.
Silence, not conversations.
Habit, not love.

And although no one likes to admit it,
many men live exactly like this:
in relationships they no longer feel but also don't leave.

Because they're afraid to start over.
Because they feel uncomfortable explaining.
Because they don't want to face loneliness.
Because they fear the financial consequences.
Because they can't handle the idea of change.
Because they don't have the courage to close a chapter.

But the truth is simple and painful:

Staying where you no longer love is not stability.
It is emotional cowardice.

How do you know you're in a relationship with no purpose?

When you are no longer partners, only roommates.

You talk about what's necessary, not what's important.
There is no mutual admiration.
There is no touch.
There is no seeking.
Arguments solve nothing.
You don't ask questions or show interest in each other.
The relationship doesn't move forward.
There are no shared dreams.
No projects.
No growth.
No excitement.
Only routine.

The relationship becomes a "functional" place:
you pay bills, organize the house, share a table... but not a life.

And the saddest part is that a lot of men know it, feel it, live it,
but keep it going because "we're fine."

No, my friend.
You're not fine.
You're stuck.

Why does a man stay in a relationship that no longer works?

Comfort

He doesn't want to start over.
He prefers surviving to rebuilding

Fear of change

A new life terrifies him because he doesn't know how to navigate it.

Lack of purpose

A man without direction doesn't know where to go…
so he doesn't move.

Guilt

He feels responsible for the pain he might cause by leaving…
but not responsible for the pain his presence is causing.

The illusion of stability

He believes "as long as there are no fights, everything is fine."
But indifference also destroys.

Emotional routine

He loves the habit, not the woman.
He misses the routine, not the relationship.

The truth men don't want to accept

Staying where you're no longer happy is also a form of betrayal.

You betray your authenticity.
You betray your dreams.
You betray your evolution.
You betray your emotional responsibility.
You betray her chance to have a real relationship.
And above all, **you betray yourself.**

A relationship without purpose eventually turns two people into strangers.
It drains your energy.
Extinguishes your emotional masculinity.
Turns you into a cold, shut-down, frustrated or indifferent man.

And she feels it.
A woman ALWAYS knows when she is no longer seen,
no longer a priority,
no longer a reason.

Can a relationship without purpose be saved?

Yes, **if love still exists.**

But it requires two things:

1. Complete honesty

Looking each other in the eyes and saying:
"We live together, but we're not living anything."

2. Real intention

Not words.
Not promises.
Not excuses.
Action.
Movement.
Concrete changes.

But there are also relationships that have finished their cycle.
That have given all they could give.
And in those cases, staying only defeats both people.

The liberating truth of this chapter

Love doesn't hurt.
What hurts is staying where love no longer lives.

Life does not stall on its own.
It stalls when *you* choose to remain frozen in a place
where you no longer grow.

A brave man knows how to let go.
A conscious man knows how to stay and build.
A wise man knows when there is nothing left to build.

Staying out of habit does not make you loyal.
It makes you a prisoner.

The right relationship awakens life.
The wrong one extinguishes it.

You deserve—and are capable of—living with purpose,
not resignation.

Real Stories of Men Trapped In Lifeless Relationships

1. The man who doesn't love her... but doesn't leave

He told me:

"I don't love her... but she has no family. I don't want to leave her alone."

They share a house.
They eat together.
They accompany each other.
But there is no intimacy.
No love.
No future.

When he tried to end it, she cried all day.
He stepped back.

His story reveals one of the quietest prisons of all:

Staying out of pity also destroys two people.

2. The man living in an empty marriage "for the kids"

A dentist told me:

"My life is total boredom. There's no connection. We're only together for the children."

Routine keeps them under the same roof.
Fear of hurting the kids keeps him there.

But emotionally, he left long ago.

A woman needs to:

- feel seen
- feel heard
- feel desired
- feel safe
- feel valued
- feel at ease
- feel important
- feel respected

Do you know what turns a woman off instantly?
A man who only thinks about his own pleasure.

Do you know what turns her on?
A man who takes his time.

Intimacy starts hours before... not 5 minutes before

Women fall in love with simple things:

- a message
- a slow kiss
- a soft look
- a deep hug
- a phrase that makes her feel wanted
- a sincere "you look beautiful today"

A woman gives herself when she feels no pressure.
When she feels no rush.
When she feels connection.

Female seduction is NOT physical.
It's emotional.

The most common male mistake: "She adapts to me."

Some men believe:

- if he's in the mood, she should be too
- if he wants it fast, she should want it fast
- if he doesn't need affection, she doesn't either
- if he feels little, she feels little

NO.

A woman is not a mirror of a man.
She functions differently, feels differently, needs differently.

A man who doesn't understand this → **fails, even when he thinks he's succeeding.**

A woman's body is NOT a switch... it is a map

And to read that map, you need:

- patience
- curiosity
- presence
- respect
- intention

A woman needs:

- touch
- kisses
- time
- rhythm
- foreplay

- communication
- softness at first
- intensity when she's ready

Most women don't enjoy intimacy because:

- he goes too fast
- he goes straight to the point
- he doesn't observe her body
- he doesn't ask
- he doesn't breathe
- he doesn't listen

Yes: listening is part of intimacy.

Premature ejaculation: what no one dares tell men

It is not shame.
It is not weakness.
It is not failure.

It is **anxiety**.

And it improves with:

- breathing
- slow rhythm
- conscious pauses
- focusing on her
- simple exercises
- releasing the pressure to "perform"

Most men make it worse because they:

- pretend it didn't happen
- make awkward jokes

- disconnect emotionally
- get frustrated
- blame her

A brave man doesn't run from the problem,
he works on it.

Women who've never had an orgasm are NOT "broken"

What's broken is:

- communication
- sexual education
- male ego
- lack of emotional connection
- rushing
- absence of foreplay
- zero sensitivity to her body and timing

A woman can be with a man for years… and never feel true fulfillment.
And he believes she has.

Because many women fake it to avoid hurting him.

This chapter is for men to wake up:

If she doesn't speak, **ASK.**
If she doesn't react, **OBSERVE.**
If she doesn't flow, **ADJUST.**

Intimacy is a dance, not a chore.

What truly satisfies a woman (and almost none know)

What melts her is NOT:

- size
- strength
- speed
- duration
- performance
- acrobatics

What turns her on is:

- slow kisses
- hands that explore
- soft words
- attention to detail
- synchronized breathing
- rhythm that matches hers
- emotional language
- a patient man
- a man who doesn't rush
- a man who is present

Women get excited by **connection**, not contact.

The most powerful truth

A satisfied woman:

- loves more
- trusts more
- opens more
- gives herself more
- becomes more affectionate

- becomes more confident
- becomes more passionate

Because she's not "fulfilling a duty."
She's **enjoying it.**

Intimacy does NOT end when you finish

This is essential.

The immature man:

- rolls over
- falls asleep
- goes to the bathroom
- disconnects

The conscious man:

- embraces
- caresses
- holds her
- thanks her
- stays present

Intimacy is an emotional circle, not a race.

Satisfying a woman doesn't take away your masculinity... it multiplies it

A man who knows how to satisfy a woman:

- doesn't need ego
- doesn't need to brag
- doesn't need to compare

- doesn't need to prove anything

His confidence shows how he makes her feel.

A man like this… is unforgettable.

Final Message for The Man Reading This

You don't need to be perfect.
You don't need complicated techniques.
You don't need to know everything.

You only need to:

- listen
- observe
- ask
- connect
- go slow
- respect her pace
- care for her emotions
- honor her body
- enjoy the process

Because satisfying a woman is NOT a physical act…
it is an act of **AWARENESS**.

"A mature man doesn't fear a woman's desire… he fears not rising to the height of her heart."

CHAPTER 25

Masculine Manners: Everyday Behaviors That Affect Attraction (More Than You Think)

Because manners are not luxurious, they are respect

There are things a man can learn.
Things he can refine.
And things that, if ignored, quietly damage attraction, respect, and connection.

This chapter is not about perfection.
It is about awareness.

A polished man is not defined by money or status, but by what he does naturally—without being asked.
His manners, habits, and daily behaviors reveal how deeply he respects himself… and how deeply he respects the woman beside him.

There are behaviors that may seem "normal," "natural," or "harmless" to you…
but that are deeply unattractive and uncomfortable for many women.

Not because women are demanding.
Not because they want perfection.
But because manners are a basic form of respect.

Table manners matter

Yes, they do.

Talking with food in your mouth, chewing loudly, slurping, licking fingers, or making exaggerated noises while eating is not charming or relaxed.
It is uncomfortable.

A woman does not want to feel embarrassed sitting across the table from you.

Self-control while eating communicates maturity, awareness, and respect for shared space.

Bodily control is also respect

Burping loudly in public, making jokes about it, or anticipating that others will find it amusing is not a sign of confidence; rather, it reflects a lack of social awareness.

The same applies to excessive chewing gum, especially with an open mouth, popping bubbles, or making constant noises.

These behaviors are not "masculine," "authentic," or "natural."
They are simply unpleasant.

Cleanliness and presentation are not superficial

Daily habits are not superficial, they shape how safe, comfortable, and connected a woman feels with you.

Poor hygiene, bad breath, or neglecting personal care immediately affect attraction.

This is not about luxury or brands.
It is about basic care.

A woman does not want to feel physically uncomfortable being close to you

Words and tone matter

Speaking without filters, making inappropriate jokes, or saying whatever comes to mind without considering context is not honesty.
It is lack of emotional intelligence.

Authenticity is not the same as impulsiveness.
Sincerity does not require rudeness.

A mature man thinks before he speaks, not because he is afraid, but because he understands the power of words.

Being respectful does not mean being silent.
It means knowing *how* and *when* to speak.

Social awareness and courtesy are emotional intelligence

A man who understands how to behave in public, how to respect shared environments, and how to avoid embarrassing situations creates safety.

Simple gestures—saying *please, thank you, excuse me,* or *I appreciate it*—are not formalities. They are signs of emotional maturity.

A man who expresses gratitude is not weak.
He is grounded.

Courtesy creates safety. And safety is attractive.

A woman relaxes when she knows she does not have to "manage" or "correct" her partner's behavior.

Joy is also a form of presence

A man who carries constant bitterness, criticism, or negativity slowly drains the emotional space around him.

Joy, gratitude, humor, and warmth are not childish traits.
They are signs of inner stability.

A man who knows how to enjoy life invites others to enjoy it with him.

Daily habits shape attraction

How a man cares for his body, his hygiene, his presentation, and his presence is not superficial,

it is relational.

These habits communicate:
"I am aware."
"I am intentional."
"I respect the space we share."

Attraction is sustained not by grand gestures, but by consistent respect.

When everyday behavior creates discomfort, attraction fades.

If a woman feels embarrassed, tense, or uncomfortable around you,
whether at the table, in public, or in simple daily moments,
desire slowly shuts down.
Not because she wants to punish you,
but because attraction cannot survive where there is discomfort.

This is not about being perfect

It is about being conscious.

About understanding that attraction is not built only in intimacy, conversation, or grand gestures, it is built in everyday behavior.

How you eat.
How you speak.
How you move.
How you behave around others.

Final reflection

Good manners do not make you less masculine.
They make you more grounded.

A man who respects himself naturally respects others.
And a man who understands this does not need to be asked to behave well—he simply does.

Because elegance is not about impressing.
It is about consideration.

CHAPTER 26

The Man Who Confuses Masculinity with Stubbornness

When resistance disguises itself as strength

One of the most exhausting dynamics in relationships is not cruelty, coldness, or even ego.
It is stubbornness disguised as masculinity.

This is the man who believes that "being a man" means never yielding, never listening, and never adjusting, even when doing so would clearly improve his life and his relationship.

He is not trying to hurt anyone.
But he is deeply confused.

Because he learned, somewhere along the way, that changing, cooperating, or receiving feedback means losing power.

And nothing could be further from the truth.

When opposing becomes an identity

This man often says things like:
"This is just how I am."
"That's because I'm a man."

What he is really saying is:
"I feel threatened when I'm corrected."
"I confuse guidance with control."
"I don't know how to adjust without feeling diminished."

So, he resists. Automatically.
Not because the request is unreasonable, but because compliance feels like weakness.

He rejects suggestions, corrections, and even basic cooperation, not out of strength, but out of fear of being wrong.

Stubbornness is not strength

A man who reacts defensively to simple requests is not protecting his identity—he is protecting his insecurity.

When a partner asks for something reasonable and he does the opposite, he is not asserting masculinity.
He is avoiding maturity.

True strength is not found in opposition.
It is found in discernment.

A mature man knows the difference between:

- being controlled and being considered
- being dominated and being invited to improve
- losing power and gaining harmony

Masculinity does not need constant resistance

A man who is emotionally grounded does not need to prove anything.
He does not feel smaller because he listens.

He does not feel attacked because he reflects.
He does not feel less masculine because he adjusts.

He understands that a relationship is not a battlefield.
It is a shared space.

And shared spaces require cooperation, not competition.

A man who grows... listens

The man who becomes truly respectable is the one who:

- receives feedback without feeling humiliated
- accepts correction without reacting defensively
- understands that compromise is not submission
- knows that listening does not cancel authority
- adds peace instead of tension

Masculinity is not proven by resistance.
It is revealed through emotional intelligence.

Final reflection

A man who contradicts everything does not show strength, he shows inner rigidity.
A man who knows when to listen, adjust, and collaborate shows real power.

Stubbornness does not make you a man.
Consciousness does.
Maturity does.
And self-awareness does.

CHAPTER 27

Work vs. Family: The Balance Almost No One Achieves

Truths that transform men, relationships, and lives.

There are men who believe that being providers is enough.
They think paying the bills, working hard, and "being home at night" automatically makes them good partners.

What they don't see, or don't want to see, is that they are not truly part of the life they are trying to sustain.

Some men give money, but not presence.
They provide a roof, but not peace.
They give their best energy to work… and leave only the leftovers for home.

This chapter is the invisible root of thousands of silent breakups:
emotional disconnection caused by a life where work replaces relationship.

Work does not replace presence

Many men justify themselves with phrases like:
"I work so you don't lack anything."

"Everything I do is for you."
"I'm exhausted because I sacrifice myself for this family."

Yes, work is an act of love.
But it does not replace what your partner truly needs.

A home is not sustained with money alone.
It is sustained with emotional presence.

No one misses the paycheck.
They miss the man.

Being physically home is not the same as being present

Many men say, "I'm home."
But emotionally, they are elsewhere.

They are lost in their phones.
Absent behind a screen.
Silent.
Disconnected.
Unavailable.

That kind of presence hurts more than absence.

A woman can feel when a man's body is home…
but his mind and heart are not.

When that happens, home slowly turns into a hotel:
he arrives, eats, sleeps, and leaves.

When work becomes an excuse, the relationship begins to die

Work is not the problem.
Avoidance is.

Some men use work to escape difficult conversations, emotional responsibility, conflict, participation, and self-reflection.

They hide behind "I'm busy."

But the truth is simpler and harder:
you're not busy— you're avoiding.

And while you avoid, she feels alone inside the relationship,
even when you're sitting right next to her.

Relationships don't end because of one big mistake

They end because of hundreds of small absences.

Not asking about her day.
Not listening.
Not sharing responsibility.
Not participating.
Not connecting.

Relationships don't die when someone leaves.
They die when someone stops being present.

Being a provider does not automatically make you a good partner

Many men believe paying the bills means they are fulfilling their role.

But providing is only one part of partnership.

Some use money as a shield—to justify emotional distance, lack of support, irresponsibility, and even betrayal.

She did not fall in love with a salary.
She fell in love with a man.

She wants the man, not the paycheck.

Balance is not found. It is built.

Men wait for the perfect moment:
"When work slows down."
"When I'm less stressed."
"When I have more time."

That moment does not exist.

Balance begins the day you decide to create it—
by setting boundaries, disconnecting when you get home, sharing responsibility, prioritizing quality time, and protecting your emotional health.

Balance is not luck.
It is emotional discipline.

What your family truly wants from you

They don't want more things.
They want more of you.

Your attention.
Your calm.
Your affection.

Your laughter.
Your presence.

Families don't remember the gifts.
They remember how you made them feel.

The final truth

Work gives you lifestyle.
Family gives you meaning.

If you keep prioritizing the first over the second,
one day you may realize you have no one left to share your success with.

Real masculine success is not measured by money, titles, or hours worked.
It is measured by what you build inside your home:
your relationship, your children, your peace.

Balancing your life is not a luxury.
It is one of your greatest emotional responsibilities.

CHAPTER 28

Men Who Erase Themselves: When Losing Yourself Destroys the Relationship

Truths that transform men, relationships, and lives.

Many men do not lose a woman because they stop loving her.
They lose her because they stop being themselves.

They give so much.
They adapt so much.
They please so much.
They bend so deeply…
that one day they wake up as a shadow of who they once were.

And the most painful part is this:
many believe that being a "good man" means disappearing.

But a relationship is **not** built through self-erasure.
It is built through presence.

This chapter is for the men who lose themselves trying not to lose her.

When you disappear, the relationship disappears too

Some men, driven by fear, anxiety, or the need to be chosen, begin to slowly abandon themselves.
They let go of their passions.
Their interests.
Their friendships.
Their boundaries.
Their voice.
Their opinions.
Their essence.

They become what they think she wants...
and stop being who they truly are.

But a woman does not fall in love with a man without identity.
She falls in love with the man who had direction, purpose, energy, vision, and life.

When you dim yourself, masculine energy fades.
And where energy fades, attraction slowly dies.

Excessive pleasing does not build love

Being kind, attentive, and respectful is beautiful.
But becoming a man who always says:

"Whatever you want."
"Anything makes me happy."
"I'll do whatever you say."

not out of love, but out of fear of losing her,
is not devotion.

It is insecurity.

And insecurity slowly turns a man into someone who is anxious, dependent, emotionally fragile, and without identity.

A woman does not want a man who dissolves himself.
She wants a man who is grounded, conscious, stable, and able to stand on his own.

Trying too hard does not bring her closer.
It makes you invisible.

When you stop having a life of your own, admiration disappears

Love her.
Care for her.
Choose her.

But do not stop living.

A man without goals, dreams, passions, or direction becomes emotionally flat.
And attraction cannot survive where there is no movement.

A woman desires a man who grows, learns, builds, dreams, and respects himself.
Not a man who needs her to exist.

The mistake of men who erase themselves to prevent abandonment

Many men believe:

"If I give more, she won't leave."
"If I adapt to everything, we won't fight."
"If I hide my needs, she'll feel loved."

But when you stop being you to avoid losing her,
she loses the man she fell in love with.

Fear does not strengthen love.
It weakens identity.

A woman does not leave because she is unloved.
She leaves because the man she admired slowly disappeared.

When you erase yourself, she carries the emotional weight

A woman does not want to be your purpose, your identity, or your only source of value.
That is not love.

That is emotional dependence.

And dependence exhausts.

A healthy relationship needs two whole individuals—
not one whole and one empty.

Becoming yourself again is an act of love

If you have lost yourself, you can return.

Reclaim what is yours.
Your voice.
Your boundaries.
Your dreams.
Your direction.
Your self-respect.

Healthy masculinity does not disappear to please.
It expands to share.

Final truth

A man who stops being himself eventually loses everything:
his clarity,
his energy,
his purpose,
and finally, the relationship.

Do not erase yourself to love.
Do not shrink yourself to be chosen.
Do not disappear to avoid conflict.

The right woman does not want to replace you.
She wants to walk beside you.

A man who returns to himself… returns to everything.

CHAPTER 29

Money: Stronger Than Love... or Simply a Reflection of Priorities?

Truths that transform men, relationships, and lives.

Money has never been the real problem.
It never was.

What truly affects a relationship is the way a man **emotionally relates to money**—and how that relationship impacts the woman beside him.

Because money can bring a couple together…
or quietly become the weapon that erodes trust, harmony, and intimacy.

Money Reveals Values

It's not about how much you earn.
It's about what you do with what you have.

Money exposes, without filtering your maturity, your discipline, your priorities, your sense of responsibility, your respect for your partner, and your vision for the future.

Money does not define your worth as a man.
But it *does* reveal your mindset.

Money Can Unite or Divide

A relationship grows stronger when money is handled with transparency, communication, shared planning, and mutual responsibility.
When there are clear agreements, respect, and a sense of "we," money becomes a tool for building.

But when finances are surrounded by secrecy, impulsiveness, ego battles, manipulation, or power games, the relationship begins to fracture.

Money doesn't destroy relationships.
Emotional immaturity does.

When Money Becomes a Weapon

Some men use money to control, silence, humiliate, impose, or replace emotional effort.
They confuse providing with leading.
They confuse authority with insecurity.

Having money does not give you power over your partner.
Emotional stability does.

Money as a Love Language

In the hands of an emotionally healthy man, money becomes care—not control.

He provides without showing off.
Shares without humiliating.
Plans as a team.

Invests in shared dreams.
Creates safety instead of fear.

Used well, money becomes a bridge.
Used poorly, it becomes a wall.

Money Does Not Replace Presence

A man can pay for everything and still abandon emotionally.
He can provide comfort and still offer no connection.

Money never replaces love, time, respect, listening, tenderness, or emotional responsibility.

Paying bills is not the same as being present.
And providing financially does not excuse emotional absence.

Is Money Stronger Than Love?

No.

What destroys love is not money, it is irresponsibility, dishonesty, manipulation, poor habits, ego, imbalance, and lack of maturity.

It's not the money itself.
It's the man misusing it.

When the Problem Is the Man—not the Money

Money reveals character, not quantity.

There are men with plenty of money and no generosity.
And men with very little who give with their whole heart.

When promises become a way to avoid responsibility

Many men promise not to grow, but to calm conflict.
They say what she wants to hear so the discomfort goes away.
They promise tomorrow so they don't have to act today.

The promise becomes a tool of delay.
A way to buy time.
A way to keep things quiet.
A way to stay comfortable without changing anything.

Over time, the woman realizes something painful:
his words are not bridges… they are distractions.

The man who lives in intention, not in action

Some men genuinely believe their promises when they make them.
They imagine themselves changing.
They visualize a better version of who they could be.

But imagination is not commitment.

They promise from emotion, not from structure.
From desire, not from discipline.
From fantasy, not from self-awareness.

And so, their life is filled with unfinished plans, half-kept words, and repeated apologies.

Not because they are evil…
but because they are immature.

When words lose value, admiration disappears

A woman can forgive mistakes.
She can forgive confusion.
She can forgive imperfection.

What she cannot forgive for long is inconsistency.

Every broken promise slowly erodes something essential:
trust, admiration, safety, and emotional connection.

She stops believing him.
Then she stops relying on him.
And eventually, she stops seeing him as a man she can build with.

Not because she stopped loving...
but because she stopped trusting.

A man's word is his character

A promise is not a sentence.
It is a commitment.

When a man breaks his word repeatedly, he is not just disappointing someone else,
he is weakening himself.

Because a man who cannot trust his own word
cannot expect anyone else to trust him either.

Broken promises steal more than moments.
They steal credibility.
They steal leadership.
They steal respect.

And eventually, they steal the relationship.

What a mature man understands

A grown man does not promise to impress.
He promises only what he can sustain.

He knows his limits.
He respects his capacity.
He understands that silence is better than an empty promise.

And if he cannot deliver, he says so—
clearly, honestly, without excuses.

That is not weakness.
That is integrity.

The truth that separates boys from men

Anyone can promise beautifully.
Only a mature man delivers consistently.

Masculinity is not proven through words.
It is proven through coherence.

Through showing up.
Through following through.
Through becoming reliable.

Because a man who does what he says
does not need to convince anyone of his worth.

His actions speak for him.

And that…
is the kind of man a woman can trust, respect, and build a life with.

CHAPTER 31

Men Who Lie Out of Habit: The double emotional life that destroys trust

Truths that transform men, relationships, and lives.

There are men who do not lie to protect.
They do not lie out of fear in the moment, nor out of insecurity in a specific situation.

They lie because lying has become their way of existing.

Their identity is so entangled with masks, half-truths, and edited versions of themselves that they no longer know where honesty ends and performance begins. Over time, truth becomes uncomfortable, and the lie feels safer.

This chapter is for those men.

Lying as an emotional refuge

The habitual liar is not clever.
He is afraid.

Afraid of confrontation.
Afraid of consequences.

Afraid of being seen as he truly is.
Afraid of losing control.
Afraid of disappointing others—or himself.

Instead of facing what needs to be worked on, he hides behind excuses, omissions, and promises he has no intention or structure to fulfill. The lie becomes a refuge, a place where he feels temporarily protected.

But what begins as refuge ends as prison.

Because a man who lies constantly is always alert, always guarding his story, always remembering what version he told to whom. And that internal tension slowly erodes his peace.

The double emotional life

This is not only about lying to a woman.
It is about living divided.

Saying "I'm fine" while carrying unresolved pain.
Saying "I love you" without knowing how to love.
Saying "I'll change" while repeating the same behaviors.
Saying "you can trust me" while hiding parts of the truth.
Showing one face to the world and another behind closed doors.

The double emotional life is exhausting.
One part of him wants to grow.
The other refuses to leave the comfort of the shadows.

This inner contradiction is what destroys his relationships, and eventually, himself.

The damage caused by habitual lying

When a man lies repeatedly, he does not just break trust.
He destroys emotional safety.

His partner begins to doubt her own intuition.
She lives alert, reading between lines, questioning details, feeling anxiety where peace should exist. Love becomes vigilance.

Over time, affection weakens. Admiration fades. Respect wears away.

When respect fades, love loses its foundation.

A persistent lie not only ends relationships; it also undermines credibility, affecting how others perceive you and how you view yourself.

Why he lies so much

A man who lies out of habit avoids reality.
He wants the benefits of being perceived as a good man without doing the inner work required to become one.

Often, he learned early on that truth leads to conflict, rejection, or punishment. The lie became his emotional language, his way of surviving.

In many cases, his self-esteem is so fragile that he needs a false version of himself to feel valuable. The lie makes him feel bigger, safer, more in control.

But beneath every lie, there is always the same truth:
he is avoiding himself.

And slowly, without realizing it, he begins to destroy the very life he is trying to protect.

Can he change?

Yes, but not through promises.

Real change never begins with speeches.
It begins with honesty.

With admitting, without excuses or decoration, that lying has become a pattern and that it is ruining his life.

It continues with identifying the emotion he is avoiding fear, shame, rejection, failure, feeling small. The lie is only a bandage; beneath it, there is always a wound.

Change requires responsibility. Not blaming childhood, parents, partners, or circumstances. He chooses to lie. And only he can choose to stop.

Integrity is practiced daily, through small, consistent actions backed by truth. Especially when telling the truth makes him look imperfect.

That is the real test of honesty.

The truth few men want to accept

A woman does not leave because of truth.
She leaves because of accumulated lies.

She leaves because of incoherence, broken promises, and emotional exhaustion. Because she no longer knows who she is with.

A man can make mistakes, everyone does.
But the man who lies without remorse, who manipulates trust, who fabricates versions of himself, pushes the woman away long before she physically leaves.

By the time she walks out, she already left emotionally.

The man who chooses truth

When a man abandons lying, something powerful happens.

He becomes reliable.
He becomes grounded.
He becomes respected.
He becomes credible.
He becomes free.

Because true masculine strength is not found in intimidation, harshness, or arrogance.
It is found in the courage to look at oneself in the mirror without disguises.

A man who chooses truth does not become perfect.
He becomes real.

And that is where real connection begins.

CHAPTER 32

The Double Game: Husband at home, single outside

Truths that transform men, relationships, and lives.

There are men who are not divided between two women.
They are divided between two versions of themselves.

The man they perform at home
and the man they allow themselves to be when no one is watching.

Because having friends, hobbies, and a social life is healthy.
Living two parallel emotional lives is not.

One life is responsible, predictable, and familiar.
The other is playful, available, and emotionally unattached.

This chapter is not an attack.
It is a mirror.

The double game does not begin with infidelity

It begins with ego.

A man who lives a double life is not only looking for pleasure.
He is looking for validation.

He wants to feel admired without effort.
Free without losing comfort.
Desired without responsibility.
He wants the stability of a family and the thrill of being "available."

The truth is uncomfortable, but simple:
a man who needs two lives is a man who has not learned to live peacefully with himself.

So, he escapes into fantasies, attention, and secret spaces where he can feel powerful,
instead of confronting the emptiness he avoids at home and within.

When "innocent activities" become emotional cover

The double life rarely announces itself loudly.
It hides behind normality.

Social outings.
Extended schedules.
Sudden need for privacy.
Hours offline.
Conversations that become guarded.

The problem is not the activity.
It is the intention behind it.

When transparency disappears, trust follows.

Why some men choose to live divided

Not because they are free.
But because they are afraid.

CHAPTER 33

Silent Violence: Yelling, Humiliation, and Fear in Disguise

Truths that transform men, relationships, and lives

Violence doesn't always leave bruises.
Sometimes it leaves silence.
It leaves sleepless nights.
It leaves a broken sense of self-worth.
It leaves a fear a woman cannot explain.
It leaves a deep wound no one sees… except the one who suffers it.

Many men believe they are "not violent" because they've never hit a woman.
But violence doesn't begin with hands.
It begins with the voice.
With words.
With attitudes.
With the way a man uses, or abuses, his emotional power.

This chapter is for the men who say they are "correcting," "teaching," or "setting order" …
when in reality, they are suffocating the soul of the woman who lives with them.

The violence you don't see, but she feels

Silent violence manifests in various forms:

- Yelling that leaves her immobilized
- Humiliation that causes her to question her self-worth
- Remarks that gradually diminish her sense of value
- Sarcasm cloaked as humor

Silence used as a form of punishment.

It doesn't take bruises to cause damage. It takes repetition.
And many men repeat these behaviors daily without seeing it,
or worse, without wanting to accept it.

When the man becomes the fear inside his own home

The woman loses her identity:

- She begins to walk with caution
- Carefully selects her words
- Breathes gently to avoid irritating him
- Steers clear of subjects that could trigger his anger
- Experiences guilt for actions she didn't commit
- Offers apologies even when she isn't at fault

Emotional violence transforms the home into a perilous environment. She remains uncertain of which version of him will emerge.

That is not love.
That is control.
And control never builds,
it always destroys.

Why does he act this way?

Not as a justification, but an explanation.

An emotionally violent man often acts this way due to his inability to cope with frustration. He may have learned that yelling leads to compliance, and violence was a normalized part of his upbringing. Feeling inferior, he resorts to exerting power to regain a sense of balance, lacking effective communication skills. For him, authority and intimidation are intertwined concepts, which unfortunately lead him to project his unresolved issues onto her.

None of this is an excuse. It is a warning:
if he doesn't work on this, the pattern destroys everything it touches.

Humiliation: the favorite weapon of the insecure man

Humiliation is the most cowardly form of emotional violence.

And it often sounds like this:

- "You're useless."
- "Who's going to want you?"
- "You're dramatic."
- "You're crazy."
- "Without me, you're nothing."

The man who humiliates is not strong.
He is small.
So small he needs to destroy someone else to feel big.

And by destroying a woman's self-esteem...
he also destroys his chance of being loved in a healthy way.

Yelling: the most honest confession of a man who cannot manage his emotions

Yelling is not authority.
Yelling is emotional incompetence.

When a man yells, what he is really saying is:

- "I don't know how to talk."
- "I don't know how to resolve."
- "I don't know how to control my emotions."
- "I feel small and I'm dumping it on you."

The man who yells loses respect, loses admiration...
and loses the love he claims to want.

Can a man like this change?

Yes.
But *not* with empty promises or repeated apologies.

He only changes if:

he admits he is violent
he stops justifying his actions
he commits to never yelling again
he learns to communicate without destroying
he seeks professional help
he works on emotional regulation
he repairs with actions, not speeches

Because apologizing and repeating the behavior is NOT change.
It is emotional manipulation.

The truth he needs to hear

A woman who exists in fear does not truly love, she merely endures.

She is not in a partnership; instead, she feels confined.

The man who instills fear in his partner does not have a family; he possesses emotional captives.

Then one day, quietly, without shouting, without theatrics, and without notice… she walks away.

When a weary woman discovers tranquility in a new place, she never goes back to the torment she fled.

The man who decides not to repeat the story

When a man relinquishes violence, he transforms into something remarkable:

- A man who listens
- A man who shows care
- A man who protects without overpowering
- A man who leads without raising his voice
- A man who loves without causing pain

That man is worth something.
That man exists.
That man can look at his partner, his children, and himself without shame.

CHAPTER 34

The New Infidelity: Social Media, Likes, and Secret Emotional Lives

Truths that transform men, relationships, and lives

Infidelity no longer hides in motels, suspicious schedules, or midnight calls.
Today it hides where no one looks:
in the pocket, turned face-down on the table.

It hides in a deleted message.
In an emoji sent "as a joke."
In a photo replied to with intention.
In conversations that begin innocently… and end up destroying an entire relationship.

Modern infidelity doesn't leave marks on the skin.
It leaves marks on the soul.

Modern infidelity begins long before crossing a physical line

It begins in small gestures he prefers to call "nothing":

- constant likes on the same woman's posts

- suggestive emojis
- messages he sends only when his partner isn't there
- conversations he deletes
- contacts saved under fake names
- hidden photos
- "friends" with emotional access his partner knows nothing about

That is emotional infidelity.
And emotional infidelity today destroys more relationships than physical cheating,
sometimes faster, sometimes deeper.

Because it lives in secrecy… while he swears, he's "not doing anything wrong."

Why do they do it? The reason most will never admit

It's not temptation.
It's not beauty.
It's not boredom.

It's something far more painful:

- they need to feel validated
- they seek attention they haven't earned
- they crave easy admiration to soothe their emptiness
- they enjoy feeling desired without responsibility

In simple terms:

Digital infidelity is emotional immaturity with internet access.

The favorite self-deception: "she's just a friend"

The modern cheater's favorite phrase.

But let's be clear:

No man deletes innocent conversations.
No man hides a healthy friendship.
No man erases messages that "mean nothing."
No man silences notifications by accident.

When he says, "she's just a friend," but...

- he checks her photos
- comments on her stories
- writes to her when he feels lonely
- seeks her out after arguing with his partner
- tells her things he would never say in front of his wife

That is NOT friendship.
That is emotional flirting.
And yes,
it is infidelity, even without physical contact.

The digital double standard

According to them, they're "not doing anything wrong" because "they haven't touched anyone."

But some betrayals require no skin:

- emotional disloyalty
- romantic attention directed at someone else
- mental time stolen from the relationship
- intimacy inside a private chat

- desire disguised as likes

A woman always feels it.
She doesn't need proof.
She doesn't need to check the phone.
Her intuition recognizes when he is no longer truly hers…
even if he sleeps beside her.

The modern excuse: "that's just how social media is"

No.
That's how men without boundaries behave.

Because a mature man:

doesn't play double
doesn't feed other women's illusions
doesn't expose himself to unnecessary temptation
doesn't seek validation from strangers
doesn't do anything he wouldn't do in front of his partner

Fidelity is not about surveillance.
It's about character.

Can a man living a digital double life change?

Yes.

But not by turning off his phone.
Not by blocking contacts.
Not by crying empty apologies.

He only changes if he:

deletes hidden conversations
stops following accounts that feed his insecure ego
rebuilds transparency
stops acting like a teenager with WiFi
faces the inner emptiness he's trying to fill
rebuilds trust with actions, not speeches

Digital infidelity isn't fixed by cleaning the phone, it's fixed by cleaning the conscience.

The truth you need to hear (even if it hurts)

A like doesn't destroy a relationship.
The intention behind the like does.

A message doesn't break a home.
The need to hide it does.

When a woman feels she is competing with the phone...
the relationship has already lost too much.

A faithful man is not the one who "doesn't get caught."
He is the one who never needs to hide.

The man who chooses digital integrity

When a man matures, something profound changes:

- he uses social media with respect
- he doesn't play with anyone's feelings
- he doesn't seek external reinforcement
- he prioritizes what truly matters
- he behaves the same in public and in private

That man is worth gold.
Not because of what he posts…
but because of what he never needs to hide.

CHAPTER 35

The Cost of Staying: Money, Fear, and Emotional Cowardice

Truths that transform men, relationships, and lives

Let's talk about the men who don't stay for love, or commitment, or family, or fear of loneliness.

They stay because getting divorced costs money.
They stay because losing assets hurts more than losing the woman.
They stay because their real bond is not emotional… it's financial.

This chapter is for them,
for the men who confuse stability with accounting,
and marriage with property management.

When marriage becomes a financial transaction

These men don't say:
"I want to save my relationship."
They say:
"Divorce would be too expensive."

They don't fight for the couple.
They fight for the assets.

When a man values the car more than the woman beside him,
the marriage stops being a union and becomes a contract,
one where the partner is the "financial risk" he refuses to take.

If losing money hurts more than losing her,
we already know how much love weighs in his life.

The double life falsely labeled as 'stability'

Many of these men:

- aren't faithful
- aren't present
- aren't honest
- aren't true partners

But they *are* "strategic."

They maintain a perfect image at home
while living like emotional bachelors outside.

Why don't they separate?

Because divorce means:

- splitting assets
- alimony
- child support
- loss of control
- exposing their mistakes

So, they prefer deceiving their wives… rather than facing a judge.

The emotional injustice the woman endures

The wife is trapped in a relationship where:

- there is no love
- no respect
- no attention
- no connection
- no shared dreams
- no growth

But she hears phrases like:

"Right now, I can't leave you."
"When I sort out my finances, we'll see."
"Everything is under my name."
"If I divorce you, I lose everything."

She slowly breaks down emotionally while waiting for a change
he will **never** make—
because his priority isn't rebuilding the relationship…
but protecting his estate.

The real root of the problem: it's not love, it's identity

Here comes the deeper truth most men will never admit:

Some don't stay for money…
They stay because **without** that money they feel they are nothing.

For them:

assets = identity
properties = masculinity

bank accounts = self-worth
status = "who I am"

Losing assets, to them, isn't losing things… it's losing themselves.

And a man who only has value through what he *owns*
does not know how to love from who he *is*.

The silent price he does pay (even if he thinks he doesn't)

He may think he "won" by avoiding divorce,
but he pays a devastating price:

- he loses peace
- loses dignity
- loses freedom
- loses integrity
- loses self-respect
- loses growth
- loses any chance at a healthy relationship
- loses the woman quietly… long before she leaves

A man who stays for financial interest becomes a prisoner of his own fear.
The prison is not the wife.
The prison is his cowardice.

Can a man like this change?

Yes,
but not through money.

Through **consciousness**.

He must face difficult truths:

financial stability doesn't heal emotional emptiness
staying for assets is another form of abandonment
honesty is worth more than a house
pretending "stability" destroys more than divorce
emotional freedom sometimes has a price... but it's worth paying

Real change begins when he stops protecting his possessions
and starts protecting his soul.

The truth he needs to hear

A man can keep:

- his house
- his cars
- his accounts
- his status
- his "comfort"

...and still lose his entire emotional life.

He can live in a big house while living a small life.
He can keep his wealth intact while his heart falls apart.

That is not success.
That is emotional poverty with a pretty façade.

What women never say out loud... but always feel

A woman beside a man who refuses to divorce for financial reasons does **not** feel:

- chosen

- loved
- valued
- partnered

She feels:

- like a burden
- like an obstacle
- like a transaction
- like a financial risk
- like a number in his calculation

And when a woman stops feeling like a person
and starts feeling like a cost… the love dies in silence.

The man who chooses courage

An honorable man:

takes responsibility
faces consequences
stops hiding
acts with integrity
puts his life in order with truth
stops using money as a shield
chooses emotional freedom over financial convenience

Because loving doesn't always cost money…
but lying, manipulating, and staying for financial interest,
that always ends up being very expensive.

CHAPTER 36

Your Sex Does Not Make You More of a Man: When Performance Replaces Presence

Truths that transform men, relationships, and lives.

Sit down, because this isn't soft. But if you have the courage to listen, it will transform you.

Many men believe their "value" in a relationship lives between their legs. They think that as long as they perform in bed, everything else gets a free pass:

- Immaturity
- Lack of emotional responsibility
- Absence of effort
- Poor communication
- Fragile ego
- Lack of vision
- Jealousy and control
- Emotional and mental poverty

For these men, sex becomes:

- Currency
- Refuge
- Excuse
- Power tool

But here's the truth they don't want to hear:

Sex is not power – it is connection

You can last for hours. You can move heaven and earth. You can think you're an Olympic champion between the sheets.

But if your heart is closed, if your character is weak, if your ego runs your life, if your emotional maturity is minimal…

She doesn't admire you. She doesn't respect you. She's not choosing *you*. She's choosing the *sensation.*

And that, my friend… always ends.

Female desire is not sustained by the body alone. It is sustained by emotion, treatment, admiration, and connection.

A man without substance, no matter how "good in bed", eventually becomes empty.

If you use sex as punishment, you're not dominant – you're immature

The man who says:

- "I'm not having sex with you until I want to."
- "You'll just have to deal with it."

- "I'll deny you so you can learn."

He is not macho. Not dominant. Not strong.

He is:

- A vengeful boy
- Insecure
- Emotionally limited
- Manipulative
- And honestly… foolish

Because some men believe withholding sex gives them power. But a mature woman punishes with something far stronger: *emotional distance.*

And when the connection disappears… that relationship is already dying emotionally.

If you think your performance is enough to keep her, you don't understand women

A woman stays with a man who:

- Cares for her
- Listens
- Respects her
- Honors her
- Gives her peace
- Keeps his word
- Makes her feel seen
- Makes her feel valued

Sex is a complement. Not the foundation. Not the heart. Not the structure.

When your only strength is your body… you are weak.

Men who brag about their "skills" are usually covering deep insecurities

The ones who say:

- "I'm the best."
- "She won't leave me."
- "No one does what I do."

Are often the same men who:

- Don't know how to apologize
- Don't know how to solve conflict
- Don't know how to communicate without hurting
- Don't know how to give affection without conditions
- Don't know how to lead a relationship
- Don't know how to be real men

They boast about the only thing they can offer… because in everything else, they feel small.

The irony: they think they're irreplaceable — but they're not

These men believe their "sexual talent" makes them unique.

But one day, she:

- Matures
- Wakes up
- Gets tired
- Evolves
- Stops feeling
- Stops admiring

And she discovers the truth:

Physical pleasure is easy to replace. What's NOT easy to replace is:

- A strong emotional man
- A responsible man
- A man who inspires
- An honest man
- A man who brings peace

That is when they begin to cry over what they never knew how to value.

The psychological root no one explains

Many men place all their worth in sex because:

- That's where they feel in control
- That's where they feel "enough"
- That's where they're not judged
- That's where their insecurity isn't exposed
- That's where they don't need communication
- That's where they don't face their emptiness
- That's where they feel admired for a moment

But this "strength" is fragile.

As soon as the emotion fails, the desire collapses... and the man is left emotionally naked. And then he discovers he had nothing else.

Final message (the one that hurts... but wakes you up)

If your sexual energy is your biggest pride, it's because you have nothing else to offer.

A real man is not defined by how he moves in bed , but by how he moves in life.

Work on your mind.
Work on your character.
Work on your discipline.
Work on your word.
Work on your purpose.
Work on your heart.

Because the body fails.
Appearance changes.
Strength fades.

And in the end… the only thing left is who you are on the inside.

And there, my love… many end up with nothing.

CHAPTER 37

Lazy Men: The Behavior That Destroys Relationships

Truths that transform men, relationships, and lives.

There are men who aren't bad, cruel, or unfaithful. But they are something equally exhausting: **lazy**.

Laziness of the soul.
Laziness of action.
Laziness of ambition.
Laziness of love.

They live settled, resigned, numb—comfortably installed in doing the bare minimum. Expecting the relationship to sustain itself.
Expecting the woman to carry everything.
Expecting life to somehow resolve itself for them.

And then they wonder: Why she fades.
Why she's not the same.
Why one day she simply walks away.

Laziness is not rest, it's abandonment

A man can be tired. That's human. But constant laziness is something else:

- Lack of initiative
- Lack of interest
- Complacency
- Emotional neglect
- Living in "minimum effort mode"

Laziness is slow abandonment. It doesn't destroy with an explosion… It kills love drop by drop.

Nothing turns off a woman faster than feeling she does everything alone

A relationship does NOT survive on:

- "I'll do it later."
- "Tomorrow, I promise."
- "I don't feel like it."
- "You're better at that."
- "Maybe later."

Love is not carrying someone. And no woman can sustain alone what was created for two.

Love needs two hands. Not one.

Laziness isn't just physical, it's emotional

The emotionally lazy man:

- Doesn't listen

- Doesn't ask
- Doesn't propose
- Doesn't improve
- Doesn't connect
- Doesn't learn
- Doesn't grow
- Doesn't invest in the relationship

This man doesn't just fail to act... He fails to feel, to think, to evolve.

A relationship needs movement. The lazy man paralyzes it. Freezes it. Wears it down.

The real root: laziness is born from fear

Read this carefully, especially if it hits home:

These men are not lazy because they don't want to do things. They're lazy because they don't know **how** to do things.

Laziness often hides:

- Fear of failure
- Fear of not being enough
- Fear of responsibility
- Low self-esteem
- Lack of learned discipline
- Absence of healthy masculine guidance
- Childhood trauma where every effort was criticized
- Insecurity that paralyzes

It's not an excuse. It's an explanation.
But if it's not recognized, it repeats itself.

A relationship is movement. A lazy man stops everything.

A relationship needs:

- Details
- Tenderness
- Plans
- Conversation
- Initiative
- Laughter
- Cooperation
- Energy

A woman doesn't want a grown child lying on the couch. She wants a man who moves, builds, proposes, contributes.

A lazy man always has an excuse... and never a solution

- "I'm tired."
- "You do it better."
- "I'm just not like that."
- "It doesn't come naturally to me."

Sweetheart, if listening, loving, making an effort, and growing don't come easily to you, don't be taken aback when it no longer feels natural for her to remain.

Women get tired too.
Women stop insisting too.
Women stop being "born" emotionally too.

Laziness destroys female desire

This is real:

A woman doesn't lose desire "for no reason." She loses it because she is **exhausted**.

The lazy man wants sex... but doesn't want to do the emotional work that ignites it. He wants passion... but doesn't want to create connection.

Desire dies where the man disappears.

And when she leaves... that's when they wake up. Too late.

Lazy men always react on the last page of the story:

- "I didn't know it bothered you so much."
- "I really did love you."
- "I was going to change."

No. It's not that you didn't know. It's that you didn't want to move.

She didn't leave over one small thing. She left because of **accumulation**.
Because of **abandonment framed as calm**.
Because of **emotional erosion** that no one else saw.

Final message to you, lazy man with potential

You don't need to be rich.
You don't need to be perfect.
You don't need to be the best man in the world.

- Low self-esteem
- Loneliness
- Unresolved wounds
- Frustration
- Toxic pride

These are men who live from the façade… but are terrified of facing their truth.

Appearance is a costume that eventually breaks

Men who live off their image often say things like:

- "Everything's fine."
- "I can handle it alone."
- "No one will ever see me fail."
- "I don't need help."
- "Nothing affects me."

They don't say it out of strength. They say it out of fear: Fear of being vulnerable.
Fear of being truly seen.
Fear that someone might notice how insufficient they feel inside.

But something is inevitable: No one can hold a mask forever. The façade cracks.
The relationship cools.
The heart gets tired.

Because in intimacy… there are no costumes.

The problem isn't what they show, it's what they neglect

The man who lives to impress the world almost always forgets what matters most at home:

- The relationship
- Communication
- Quality time
- His mental health
- Emotional connection
- Inner growth

He's busy conquering the world... and neglecting the woman he should cherish the most.

What does a man gain by showing off a "perfect life" ... if he loses the one person who should admire him?

Ego demands perfection; life demands humanity

Men who live for appearances are terrified of being seen:

- Sad
- Confused
- Fragile
- Wrong
- Wounded

They have a giant ego on the outside... and tiny self-esteem on the inside.

They strive to project an image of invincibility, yet anything can bring them down. They desire to appear strong yet struggle with their emotions. They aim to convey a sense of security but live in a state of constant defensiveness.

These men don't connect with their partner they connect with their character

For their partner, loving a man like this is exhausting because he:

- Doesn't confide
- Doesn't express
- Doesn't trust
- Doesn't share
- Responds with pride
- Avoids depth
- Turns every comment into an attack
- Turns every mistake into drama

She ends up in love with a version of him that doesn't even exist.

And the saddest part: They don't know how to be loved... because they don't know how to be real.

Appearances are empty and emptiness is heavy

Many men have everything that looks "right":

- A career
- A nice car
- Perfect social media
- Smiling pictures
- Reputation
- Expensive clothes
- Visible success

But they lack everything essential:

- Peace
- Truth

- Authenticity
- Humility
- Emotional presence
- Purpose
- The ability to love
- The desire to heal
- The courage to look within

What they show the world weighs far less than what they hide when they are alone.

Appearance cannot sustain a home. Truth can.

One day, the woman gets tired:

- Tired of the plastic perfection
- Tired of the lack of depth
- Tired of loving someone who won't let himself be loved
- Tired of living with a man obsessed with his image but absent in his relationship

Love doesn't grow with masks.
Love grows with truth.

Final Message for the Man Who Lives as a Character

Stop acting.
Stop pretending.
Stop performing.
Stop hiding behind your ego.

While you fight to look strong… she just wants you to be real.

A man without discipline is a man without direction. You can have dreams, goals, ideas, and plans, but if you lack discipline:

- You don't advance
- You don't improve
- You don't grow
- You don't change
- You don't build anything real

Discipline is the bridge between what you say and what you do.
Between what you dream… and what you achieve.
Between what you promise… and what you fulfill.

Without discipline, your words hold little weight. Many women are growing weary of mere talk.

Real discipline includes emotional discipline

A lot of men think being disciplined means:

- Working hard
- Going to the gym
- Waking up early

That's part of it, but it's not the most important part.

Real discipline is also:

- Controlling your tone when you're angry
- Not reacting like a child when criticized
- Listening before defending
- Admitting your mistakes without excuses
- Having difficult conversations
- Facing uncomfortable truths
- Stopping the habit of blaming your past for your present

Emotional discipline is what separates a man... from a grown boy with a beard.

"That's just how I am" is a shield not an identity

When a man says:

- "I don't want to change."
- "Deal with what I give you."
- "Adapt to my flaws."
- "If you don't like it, that's your problem."

He's not being honest — he's being lazy. And no one is obligated to tolerate your lack of discipline. Not your partner.
Not your children.
Not your family.
Not the woman who loves you.

If you choose to stay "like that," then accept the consequences that come with it.

Discipline is what makes a woman admire you

It's not:

- Your money
- Your body
- Your job
- Your car
- Your charm

A woman admires a **disciplined man** because he:

- Keeps his promises
- Finishes what he starts

- Carries responsibility
- Doesn't live on excuses
- Grows and improves
- Steps up when it matters
- Leads with action, not speeches

Respect can't be demanded. It's earned through consistency.

Discipline is also breaking your patterns

A disciplined man does **not** say:

- "This is just who I am."
- "My father was like this."
- "That's how I was raised."
- "I'm impulsive — what do you expect?"

A disciplined man says:

- "I can change this."
- "I can learn this."
- "I can improve."
- "I can work on myself."

Discipline begins the moment you stop using your past as an excuse. Your past explains you — but it does not define you.

A man without discipline loses what matters most

He loses:

- Respect
- Admiration
- Trust
- Stability

- Opportunities
- His partner
- His family
- His future

And still, many keep saying: **"That's just how I am."**

Without realizing that being "like that" is what's destroying everything they love.

Final Message for the Man Who Can Do Better

Stop the excuses.
Stop the emotional laziness.
Stop fearing change.
Stop the ego that keeps you stuck.
Stop the comfort that's quietly destroying your life.

Discipline is not rigidity — it's self-respect. It is courage.
It is responsibility.
It is real masculinity.

The right woman doesn't want a perfect man.
She wants a man who is:

- Disciplined
- Committed
- Consistent
- Willing

If you choose to become that man... **your entire life will change.**

CHAPTER 40

Purpose: The Direction That Shapes Your Character

The man who builds

When a man doesn't know where he's going, everything else in his life falls apart.

A man without purpose gets lost, gets frustrated, gets angry over anything. He feels empty, becomes reactive, stuck, complacent, insecure, and emotionally unstable.

Because purpose is not a luxury. Purpose is the backbone of a man's character.

A man with purpose doesn't necessarily have everything figured out. But he has something others don't: direction, a why, an inner engine, a sense of meaning, a mission, a reason to get up.

Without purpose, a man merely exists. With purpose, a man lives.

Purpose is not a romantic dream, it's a commitment to yourself

So many men believe purpose means making money, being successful, traveling, being happy. Those things may be part of life, but they are not purpose.

Purpose is answering the question most men are afraid to face: Why am I here?

A man with purpose knows his life has direction. A man without purpose lives in survival mode — putting out fires, reacting to everything, building nothing

Purpose shapes a man's character more than any self-help book

When a man finds his purpose, he changes the way he speaks, the way he acts, the way he decides. His discipline increases. His sense of responsibility grows. His emotional strength expands. His relationship with himself transforms — and so does the way he loves.

Purpose compels him to evolve, confront his weaknesses, maintain consistency, eliminate excuses, cultivate self-discipline, and create something substantial.

A man without purpose lives reacting. A man with purpose lives choosing.

A man without purpose becomes dependent on the relationship

This point is critical.

When a man has no emotional or professional direction, he ends up depending on his partner to feel valuable. He needs constant validation. He becomes more jealous, feels inferior, demands excessive attention, wants control, and often hinders her growth.

Because when a man doesn't know who he is, the relationship becomes his only identity.

That is not love. That is a lack of purpose.

Purpose makes a man attractive without even trying

A man with purpose attracts effortlessly. You can see it in his confidence, his firmness, his focus, his clarity. You see it in his passion for life, his self-respect, his healthy ambition, and his responsibility.

He doesn't need to brag. He doesn't need to impress. He doesn't need to talk too much. His energy speaks for him.

Purpose is not found, it is built

Many men say, "I don't know what my purpose is."

Here's the truth: Purpose is not discovered. Purpose is built.

It's built when you take responsibility, truly get to know yourself, work on your wounds, stop running, do difficult things, develop discipline, and commit to something bigger than your comfort.

A man without purpose waits to feel motivated. A man with purpose acts, even when he doesn't feel like it.

Purpose turns you into a man you can be proud of

When a man finds his purpose, he stops chasing validation, approval, applause, recognition, likes, competition, and comparison.

Because he understands his value doesn't come from the outside. It comes from what he builds within.

And that changes everything. It changes his energy, his self-esteem, the way he loves, the way he decides, and his vision of the future.

Purpose not only transforms your life — it transforms you.

You're not born stable, you learn stability

Many men grew up hearing:

"Don't cry."
"Don't be weak."
"Be a man."
"Control yourself."
"Say nothing."
"Swallow it."

The result? Men who explode, shut down, run away, yell, or freeze—because they never learned to process their emotions.

Emotional stability is not genetic. It's a skill. And any man can develop it.

An unstable man makes his partner feel unsafe

A woman never knows what to expect: Today he's sweet.
Tomorrow he's cold.
In the afternoon he's angry.
At night he won't talk.
The next day he acts normal.
Then he explodes.
Then he disappears.
Then he apologizes.
Then he repeats the cycle.

That emotional rollercoaster is exhausting. It kills trust.
It kills connection.
It kills desire.

She begins walking on eggshells, measuring every word, avoiding every gesture. The relationship stops feeling like home and becomes a prison of emotional instability.

A stable man governs three fundamental areas

Mind

He doesn't believe every assumption. He doesn't get carried away by paranoia. He filters, thinks, analyzes, and then acts.

Emotion

He feels deeply, but he doesn't explode. He doesn't hurt. He doesn't shut down. He responds instead of reacting.

Action

His decisions aren't ruled by his mood. He builds; he doesn't destroy.

A stable man doesn't manipulate, threaten, or victimize himself

Unstable men often say: "I'm going to disappear." "Do whatever you want." "You'll see if you lose me." "I'm nothing." "You always do this to me." "This is just how I am."

This isn't love. It's emotional immaturity. It's manipulation. It's the absence of responsibility.

A stable man says: "I need to process this." "I'm not okay, but I'm working on myself." "Let's talk when I calm down, I don't want to hurt you."

That is emotional leadership. That is real manhood.

Stability begins when you recognize your wounds

An unstable man lives running from:

- His childhood
- His trauma

- His absent father
- Emotional neglect
- His insecurity
- His fear of abandonment

The stable man says: "This hurt me. This affects me. But I will not repeat it."

He doesn't run. He doesn't deny. He doesn't hide.

Healing is also a way of being a man.

Emotional stability makes a man irresistible

We're not talking about looks, we're talking about energy.

A stable man brings peace, safety, clarity, trust, direction, maturity, and presence.

A woman knows she can count on him. That he won't disappear. That he won't explode. That he doesn't play mind games. That he doesn't hurt and then apologize like a routine.

Stability is more attractive than muscles, money, or ego.

Stability turns a man into his best version

When a man learns to regulate his emotions, everything else begins to align:

- He makes better decisions
- He controls his impulses
- He builds healthier relationships
- He takes responsibility for his life

And this transforms: His character.
His discipline.

His self-worth.
His way of loving.
His future.

Emotional stability is one of the highest forms of masculine intelligence.

Final message for the man who wants to grow

You don't need to be perfect.
You don't need every answer.
You don't need to be strong all the time.

You only need: Calm.
Awareness.
Structure.
And the courage to feel without destroying.

Because the strong man may impress...
But the stable man stays, supports, builds, and transforms.

CHAPTER 42

How to Be a Trustworthy Man

The man who builds

Trust is not asked for.
Trust is earned, sustained, and demonstrated.

A woman may fall in love with an attractive, intelligent, passionate, or funny man… but she only stays with a **trustworthy** man.

A man can give flowers, gifts, attention, and romantic speeches. But if he's not trustworthy, he loses everything:

- Admiration
- Respect
- Connection
- Desire
- The relationship

Trust is the foundation of everything a man wants to build.

Being trustworthy is not just about not cheating, it's about being consistent

Many men believe being trustworthy simply means: "I'm not with another woman."

But trustworthiness goes far deeper.

A trustworthy man:

- Fulfills what he promises
- Tells the truth, even when it's uncomfortable
- Acts the same in public and in private
- Doesn't play with people's emotions
- Doesn't disappear when problems arise
- Doesn't change based on his mood
- Doesn't give empty promises
- Doesn't make excuses
- Doesn't manipulate
- Doesn't hide
- Doesn't live a double life

Being trustworthy is emotional coherence.
It is integrity, not surveillance.
It is character, not control.

A trustworthy man is predictable in what matters

A woman doesn't need perfection. She needs to feel safe.

She wants a man she can anticipate in the essential things:

- How he handles problems
- How he manages stress
- How he protects what he loves
- How he reacts when things get difficult
- How he responds emotionally

The unstable man surprises in negative ways.
The trustworthy man surprises through consistency.

Trust is demonstrated more in the small things than in the big ones

A trustworthy man:

- Arrives when he says he will
- Communicates when something changes
- Responds to what needs to be addressed
- Follows through without being reminded
- Respects boundaries, even when no one is watching
- Handles money responsibly
- Organizes his life with maturity
- Keeps routines and commitments

A man who doesn't honor small things... will never be able to sustain big things.

Trust breaks through silence than through lies

Men often say: "I didn't tell her so she wouldn't worry." "I handled it myself." "I didn't think it was important." "I didn't want to create a problem."

But here's the truth: **When you hide, you're the one who distrusts first.**
When you stay silent, she learns to doubt.
When you conceal, you plant insecurity.

Transparency is not a one-time act. It's a daily emotional habit.

A trustworthy man guards both his words and his actions

He does not promise love, he demonstrates it.
He doesn't say "trust me"; he gives reasons to trust.
He doesn't ask for chances, he builds worthiness.

That is manhood. That is character.

Masculine trustworthiness is also emotional stability

A trustworthy man:

- Does not explode
- Does not disappear
- Does not punish with silence
- Does not act impulsively
- Does not respond with rudeness
- Does not hurt when frustrated

Trust grows through his calm, his stability, his presence, his maturity, and his emotional steadiness.

A trustworthy man holds steady.

The man who is not trustworthy destroys everything good he does

You can be:

- A good lover
- A good provider
- A good friend
- A good partner
- A good father

But if you are not trustworthy… none of it works.

Relationships don't fall apart from lack of love.
They fall apart from lack of trust.

Without it, the bond becomes fragile, insecure, draining, and exhausting.

Final message for the man who wants to be worthy of trust

You don't need to be perfect.
You don't need to be a hero.
You don't need to be the best.

You only need to be: Clear.
Consistent.
Honest.
Stable.
Responsible.
Reliable.
Present.

Because a trustworthy man doesn't just build relationships.
He builds peace. He builds home. He builds life.

CHAPTER 43

The Importance of Your Word: What Makes You a Man

The Man Who Builds

A man's word is his identity, his signature, and his character.

The world may admire you for your looks, intelligence, money, or personality, but it only respects you if you **keep your word**.

Your word is the bridge between what you say and who you are.
Between what you promise and what you do.
Between what you dream... and what you actually build.

And here is a truth some men avoid: **Many talk too much and deliver too little.**

What You Say Creates Expectations. What You Do Creates Trust

A woman doesn't fall in love with promises.
She falls in love with **actions**.

A man may repeat a thousand times: "I'm going to change." "You can trust me." "I won't do it again." "I'll take care of it." "I've got your back."

But if he doesn't show it… his word becomes noise, not value.

When a man breaks his word, he also breaks:

- His credibility
- The respect she feels
- The emotional stability of the relationship
- The desire
- His self-esteem

Because he doesn't just fail her, **he fails himself**.

A Man Is Worth What His Word Is Worth

Your word:

- Reveals you
- Exposes you
- Defines you
- Elevates you… or sinks you

You can be charming, successful, intelligent, even extraordinary.
But if your word has no value…
you don't have much value **as a man**.

Masculinity isn't in strength. It's in steadiness.

The Man Whose Word Is Weak Lives in Excuses

Men who don't follow through always have a ready-made excuse: "I forgot." "Something came up." "I didn't think it mattered." "You know how I am." "I'll do it later."

Excuses are the crutches of the immature.
Justifications are the mask of the irresponsible.

And something is always true:

- When you fail others, you fail yourself first.
- When you promise without fulfilling, you lose the respect you demand.
- When your word means nothing... **you mean less as a partner, father, and man**.

Your Word Is an Emotional Contract

When you say **yes**, the other person organizes their life around that yes.
When you say **no**, they do the same.

That's why your word is not just sound.
It is an **emotional commitment**.

A man is measured not by what he says... but by what he sustains.

Your Word Also Includes Your Silences

You don't only break your word when you say something and don't follow through.
You also break it when you stay silent about what you should say.

Silence out of fear, convenience, or manipulation... is another form of betrayal.

Integrity lives not only in what you speak, but in what you refuse to hide.

A Strong Man's Word Builds a Home

A man of his word:

- Says little and does much

- Doesn't promise what he can't sustain
- Speaks consciously, not impulsively
- Follows through even when he "doesn't feel like it"
- Respects agreements
- Acts the same whether seen or unseen
- Honors his word above his pride

That man builds: Peace.
Security.
Admiration.
Stability.
Respect.
Real love.

A woman who has a man like this does not fear the future.

The Word You Give Today Defines the Man You Become Tomorrow

If you want to be a valuable man:

- Promise less
- Deliver more
- Commit only to what you can sustain
- Think before you speak
- Be honest, even when it's uncomfortable
- Be consistent, even when it's hard

A man without a word may have a thousand qualities…
but none will save him.

A man with a strong word may have a thousand flaws…
and he will still be respected, loved, and valued.

Because **his word represents him. Builds him. Honors him.**

Final Message

Your word is your signature.
Your character is the ink.
Your life is the document.

Be a man whose signature means more than his speech.
A man whose word builds more than it promises.
A man who leaves a mark, not excuses.

That is the man the world respects.
And that is the man a woman admires without fear.

CHAPTER 44

Masculine Responsibility: Strength Without Control

The Man Who Builds

Masculine responsibility has nothing to do with yelling, imposing, monitoring, or commanding.

Real responsibility—the kind that turns a man into a pillar, not a problem—is a blend of maturity, consistency, presence, and emotional stability.

A responsible man can be firm… but never controlling.
He can lead, but never through force.
He can protect, but never through fear or surveillance.

Today, many women are exhausted because they live with men who confuse:

- Responsibility with control
- Leadership with superiority
- Care with jealousy
- Love with vigilance

And the worst part?
They truly believe they are "doing the right thing."

Here's the truth:
Being responsible isn't about controlling others, it's about learning to control yourself.

Responsibility Begins with Self-Governance

A responsible man doesn't start by controlling his partner, his home, or his environment.
He begins by controlling:

- his emotions
- his words
- his decisions
- his character
- his time
- his money
- his reactions

A man who cannot govern himself has no emotional authority to lead a relationship.
A woman does not need an "emotional father."
She needs an adult partner.

Firmness Is Not Harshness

Some men believe that to be firm, they must be harsh.
Wrong.

Harshness intimidates.
Firmness inspires.

- Harshness says: *"This is how it is, and that's final."*
- Firmness says: *"This matters to me. Let's find a solution together."*

Firmness builds.
Harshness breaks.
Control destroys.
Responsibility unites.

A Responsible Man Doesn't Monitor, He Trusts

When a man needs to check phones, track movements, doubt without reason, or search for proof, he is confessing something:

His insecurity is in control.

Trust is not demanded.
Trust is built through consistency, transparency, and stability.

A man who trusts his woman is a man who also trusts himself.

Avoiding Problems Is NOT Maturity, it's Irresponsibility

Running from difficult conversations, delaying important decisions, or ignoring tension doesn't make a man "calm."

It makes him evasive.

Responsibility means being able to say:

"This is uncomfortable, but we will solve it together."

Avoidance is fear.
Responsibility is courage.

Coherence Is the Core of Masculine Responsibility

A responsible man doesn't need to promise much,
he needs to keep what he promises.

When a man says, "I've got it," "count on me," "I'll be there" ...
and he follows through, he becomes an emotional anchor.

When he promises and doesn't deliver, he becomes a storm.

Responsibility isn't heard.
It's felt.

A Responsible Man Brings Order, Not Chaos

Some men are hurricanes—
emotional, financial, or mental.
They complicate everything. They destabilize everything.

But a responsible man brings structure:

- He respects time
- He respects boundaries
- He pays on time
- He organizes
- He thinks before acting
- He protects his family
- He works on himself
- He knows how to sustain

It's not about perfection.
It's about consistency.

Responsibility Shows Through Respect, Not Force

Respect is the language of an adult man.
Not yelling.
Not threats.
Not silent punishment.
Not manipulation.

Choosing respect means choosing:

- Peace over pride
- Conversation over pressure
- Love over control

A responsible man never hurts the ones he loves to defend his ego.

Responsibility Is a Daily Decision

If you truly want to grow as a man, start here:

- stop blaming your childhood
- stop justifying your explosions
- stop controlling others
- stop avoiding conversations
- stop using anger as a tool
- learn to listen
- learn to apologize
- learn to follow through
- learn to respect
- learn to feel

Responsibility is not measured by what you say,
but by what you *uphold*.

Final Message

A responsible man is not the one who dominates his home...
but the one who dominates himself.

That is the man who builds.
That is the man who inspires.
That is the man who transforms his life and the lives of those around him.

CHAPTER 45

Men Who Leave Imprints, Not Wounds

The Man Who Builds

A man who builds inspires and transforms through the way he loves.

There are two kinds of men in this world:
those who enter a woman's life to add…
and those who enter only to break what they never helped build.

The first leave imprints.
The second leave scars.

And the real difference?
It's not looks.
It's not money.
It's not education.
It's not personality.

It's the kind of masculine presence they carry within.

A man who leaves an imprint is not perfect, he is conscious.
He knows that every gesture, every word, and even every silence has emotional impact.
He moves with intention.
He speaks with truth.

He loves with respect.
And he acts with integrity.

This chapter is for those men...
and especially for the ones who want to become them.

A man who leaves an imprint knows that love is proven through habits, not words

Men who hurt often speak beautifully: they promise, seduce, inspire illusions...
but they don't sustain anything.

Men who leave an imprint do the opposite:

- They speak little but follow through
- They say what they feel and live what they say
- They love through actions, not speeches
- They honor every commitment

They don't manipulate.
They don't play games.
They don't promise to conquer,
they promise because they intend to fulfill.

A woman never forgets that.

A man who leaves an imprint is mindful of how he treats a woman

He doesn't need to yell to be heard.
He doesn't need to control to feel secure.
He doesn't need to hurt to feel strong.

His strength is in his calm.
In his self-control.
In his ability to speak without destroying.

He knows how to:

- listen
- apologize
- respect boundaries
- be presence, not pressure

A man can be very "macho," very decisive, very dominant...
but if he hurts, all of that loses value.

A man who leaves an imprint stays present even on difficult days

A woman doesn't want a perfect hero.
She wants a man who doesn't run.

A man who leaves an imprint:

- stays when life gets heavy
- supports her when she cries
- faces conflict instead of avoiding it
- holds steady even when he has doubts
- loves even when he is tired

Because he understands something fundamental:
real love is also a decision, not just an emotion.

A man who leaves an imprint inspires through example, not speeches

He doesn't ask for what he doesn't practice.

He doesn't say "be strong"—he is strong.
He doesn't say "be honest"—he is honest.
He doesn't say "trust me"—he gives reasons to trust.
He doesn't say "I want a future with you"—he builds it.

Men who hurt seek admiration.
Men who leave imprints generate it naturally.

A man who leaves an imprint heals—he doesn't wound

A woman may arrive hurt, guarded, or defensive.
And he doesn't mock her, fear her emotions, or judge her.

He accompanies.
He understands.
He respects.
He supports.

Because he knows that love also means healing with her,
not opening new wounds.

A man who leaves an imprint knows when to stay... and when not to

Here is a truth many don't want to face:

Sometimes the greatest imprint a man can leave
is choosing not to continue hurting someone.

If he cannot give her what she deserves…
If his presence dims her light…
If his love no longer builds…

Then leaving is also an act of love.

A man who leaves an imprint does not destroy a woman's life—
not even by accident.
If he cannot love her well, he doesn't tie her down or confuse her.

That too leaves an imprint of respect.

Every woman feels the difference

The body knows.
The soul recognizes it.

A man who leaves an imprint is not perfect,
but his presence carries a different energy:

- calm
- consistency
- steadiness
- respect
- intention
- light

You can see it in his eyes, in his tone, in his gestures.
You can feel it in the peace he brings,
not the chaos he avoids or creates.

Becoming that man isn't a talent it's a choice

No one is born knowing how to love.
But every man can learn.

He may have wounds, traumas, mistakes, fears...
but if he chooses growth, healing, and transformation,
then he can become the man no one forgets:

The man who builds.
The man who adds.
The man who transforms.
The man who leaves imprints... not wounds.

"That is the man women remember, not because he promised much, but because he built more than he ever promised."

CHAPTER 46

How to Build a Healthy Relationship: Step by Step

The guide every man needs (but almost none considers)

A healthy relationship is not improvised.
It's not luck.
It's not chemistry.
It's not "if it works, it works."

That phrase is the favorite excuse of immature men who don't understand that love is something you **build**, not something that randomly happens.

A healthy relationship is built the same way a home, a business, or a life is built.
And the man who understands this, stops being just a partner…
and becomes an emotional teammate, a co-creator, a true team.

Here begins what no one taught them, but every man should know.

1. Everything starts with you: the man you are determines the relationship you have

Before looking at the woman, before demanding, before asking for what you don't give...
look at yourself.

You cannot have a healthy relationship with another human being
if you maintain a toxic relationship with yourself.

An insecure man controls.
A man without self-esteem wounds.
An unstable man confuses.
A selfish man exhausts.
A healthy man connects.

That is the difference between **building** and **destroying**.

2. Adult communication: clarity without yelling, honesty without attacking

A healthy relationship does NOT run on:

- hints
- long silences
- "it's nothing" when it is
- sarcasm
- guessing games

A healthy man:

- speaks without yelling
- expresses without hurting
- listens without interrupting
- tells the truth even when it's uncomfortable

Clarity doesn't create problems.
It prevents wars.

3. Love is not control: it is giving freedom with healthy boundaries

Love has space.
Space for her to be herself.
For you to be yourself.
To grow individually without fear.

Love that suffocates is not love, it is fear concealed.

A man who builds a healthy relationship does NOT:

- check her phone
- control her social media
- censor her clothes
- limit her friendships
- demand reports
- give "permissions"

That man is not caring—he is policing.
And policing is not love.

Freedom does not destroy relationships.
Control does.

4. Trust is built, not demanded

No man has the right to say "trust me"
if his actions say otherwise.

Trust grows from:

- consistency
- respect
- truth
- responsibility
- emotional stability

A trustworthy man does not beg for trust—
he **inspires** it.

5. Emotional details: the real pillars of connection

Men think details are flowers and gifts.
No.

The real details are emotional:

- looking at her when she talks
- listening without defending yourself
- recognizing her efforts
- noticing her sadness
- appreciating her presence
- showing interest in her world
- reminding her she is chosen

Attention builds.
Indifference destroys.

6. Solve, don't accumulate: the difference between peace and war

A healthy relationship does NOT:

- keep score
- revive old fights
- throw indirect comments
- weaponize the past
- punish with silence

Healthy couples talk.
Even when it hurts.
Even when it's uncomfortable.

Resolving things on time is the vaccine against resentment.

7. Be a partner, not a parent; be a teammate, not a boss

A mature relationship feels like this:
"We are two adults walking together."

Not a father with a daughter.
Not a boss with an employee.
Not a coach with a student.

A healthy relationship is built on:

- respect
- balance
- emotional equality
- mutual admiration
- shared decisions

No one commands.
Both build.

8. A healthy relationship is not abandoned when it gets uncomfortable

Many men run the moment the relationship becomes real:

- deep emotions
- responsibility
- commitment
- difficult conversations
- repairing wounds

A healthy man:

- stays
- faces
- talks
- repairs
- grows
- supports

He does not disappear when she needs him the most.

9. Loving with maturity: you are responsible for yourself, not for your voids

A healthy relationship is not:

"Make me happy."
"Fill my emptiness."
"Heal me."
"Meet all my needs."

That is ego, not love.

Mature love says:

"Let's walk together."
"I work on myself so I can love you better."
"I strengthen myself so I can support you."
"We grow as a team."

That is the kind of love that transforms,
not the kind that drains.

10. Healthy relationships leave imprints... not scars

When a man loves well, a woman blooms:

She breathes differently.
Trusts differently.
Walks differently.
Loves differently.

Because peace is the first symptom of healthy love.
And an emotionally mature man gives something priceless:
emotional safety.

CHAPTER 47

Cold Emotional Men: Zero Details, Zero Romance, Zero Connection

The man who builds

There are men who don't yell, don't hit, don't cheat, and don't humiliate... but they hurt in a silent way: **through absence**.

They hurt with coldness.
With indifference.
With that emotional silence that turns everything gray.

They're not violent, but they're not loving either.
They don't cause harm, but they don't do good.
They don't wound... but they don't make the woman beside them feel alive.

And yes:
Emotional coldness is also a form of abandonment.

The man who doesn't feel... or doesn't know how to feel

Many grew up believing that:

- romance is silly

- details are "women's stuff"
- affection is shown by working hard and that's it

But here is the truth they need to consider:

If a man doesn't know how to show love, his partner cannot feel loved.

Yet he expects her to be satisfied.

The problem isn't that he doesn't bring flowers.
The problem is that **he doesn't think about her**.

She changes her hair — he doesn't notice.
She wears a new perfume — he doesn't smell it.
She dresses sexy — he doesn't blink.
She's sad — he doesn't ask.
She's exhausted — he doesn't help.

That's not forgetfulness.
That's chronic emotional disconnection.

Romance is not bought — it's built

It's not about fancy dinners or expensive gifts.
It's about **emotional presence**:

A glance.
A long hug.
A message out of nowhere.
A "tell me about your day".
A "I'm with you".

Cold men think those things "don't matter" ... until one day she gets tired and he asks:

— "What happened? I didn't do anything..."

Exactly.

You didn't do anything.
And nothing hurts more than that.

Men who give no affection... but want to know EVERYTHING

Control disguised as concern

There is a type of man who doesn't hug, but interrogates.
He gives no affection, but demands explanations.

- Who called you?
- Why did you get dressed up?
- Where were you?
- Who texted you?
- Why are you late?

He doesn't notice her new haircut...
but he checks her phone.

He doesn't say "you look beautiful" ...
but he does say "who are you trying to impress?"

He isn't just cold.
He's **cold and controlling**.

And that combination becomes an emotional prison.

Men who "don't know how to give" ... except when it benefits them

Here comes a truth that hurts but frees:

Coldness is not a personality trait. It's a choice.

A man *can* be thoughtful… **when he wants to be**.
He *can* be romantic… **when he cares**.
He *can* give attention… **when he fears losing someone**.

Because for other things, he *does* have energy:

- he takes care of his car
- he gets excited about sports
- he memorizes stats
- he plans outings with friends
- he stays up late for video games or work

He has passion, interest, focus…
just **not for her**.

A woman doesn't need a man who "isn't bad."
She needs a man who is **good to her**.

The final truth for them

Men:

Women don't expect perfection.
They expect **presence**.

Romance isn't childish;
it's emotional maturity.

Details aren't expenses;
they're a language.

Attention isn't control;
it's care.

A cold man doesn't lose his partner overnight.
He loses her slowly:

Every time he ignores.
Every time he doesn't notice.
Every time he doesn't ask.
Every time he doesn't touch.
Every time he doesn't appreciate.

Until one day she leaves.
Not because she stopped loving him...
but because she got tired of not feeling loved.

PART FOUR

REAL TRANSFORMATION

Where You Come from Does Not Define Where You Can Go

Wounds they didn't choose.
Wounds they didn't deserve.
Wounds no one ever taught them how to understand—let alone heal.

This chapter is for the man who wants to change,
but feels that his past keeps sabotaging every step.

Wanting to Change Is Not Weakness It Is Awareness

Many men were taught that changing means losing strength, authority, or masculinity.
They were told that to grow is to "give in," to heal is to "be soft," and to look within is to "break."

But the truth is the opposite.

The man who refuses to change is not strong, he is afraid.
The man who chooses growth is courageous.

It takes far more strength to face your own character than to pretend nothing is wrong.
It takes more masculinity to heal than to hide.

Wanting to change is not weakness.
It is consciousness waking up.

Why Wounds Block Change

A wounded man doesn't always look wounded.

Sometimes he looks confident.
Sometimes arrogant.
Sometimes cold.
Sometimes controlling.

Sometimes explosive.
Sometimes distant.

But inside, he lives in constant defense mode.

Because unhealed wounds don't disappear, they react.

The man who yells is not "bad." He is wounded.
The man who controls is not dominant. He is insecure.
The man who avoids intimacy is not indifferent. He is afraid.
The man who shuts down emotionally is not strong. He is protecting himself.
The man who repeats the same mistakes is not stupid—he is unconscious.

Your reactions are not your character.
They are your defense mechanisms.

Until you heal, your wounds will keep responding for you.

You Don't Lack Love You Lack Healing

Many men believe that to feel better they need more of something outside themselves:

More control.
More money.
More recognition.
More power.
More women.
More authority.

But what they truly need is internal:

Inner peace.
Emotional security.
Self-worth.
Stability.

Self-forgiveness.
Freedom from the past.

A man does not improve by accumulating more.
He improves by healing more.

The First Step Is Not Understanding It Is Acceptance

Before change begins, a man must face a difficult truth:

"What I'm doing is not working."

Accepting this does not humiliate you.
It liberates you.

What you deny controls you.
What you justify continues.
What you accept becomes transformable.

Change does not start with explanations.
It starts with responsibility.

You Can't Change What You Don't Know

A lot of men are not bad—they are unaware.

They don't realize that they:

- speak in ways that wound
- love from fear
- control without intending to
- hurt without meaning to
- repeat patterns learned in childhood
- carry emotional wounds they never healed

To change, you need something no one may have taught you:

Introspection.

The courage to ask yourself:

- Why do I react this way?
- What am I protecting?
- What fear is governing my behavior?
- What am I repeating from my past?
- Which part of me never matured emotionally?

A man who asks these questions has already begun to change.

Healing Is Not About Blame It Is About Responsibility

Your wounds are not your fault.
But they are your responsibility.

You didn't choose your childhood.
You didn't choose abandonment, neglect, or emotional absence.
You didn't choose trauma or silence.

But today, you can choose not to repeat it.

Healing does not mean saying, "Everything was fine."
Healing means saying, "This will no longer rule my life."

That is maturity.
That is integrity.
That is real masculinity.

Change Is a Process, not a Switch

No one becomes a new man overnight.

But you can make new decisions today.

If yesterday you reacted, today you pause.
If yesterday you yelled, today you breathe.
If yesterday you avoided, today you stay.
If yesterday you ran, today you face.

Change happens in small, consistent actions, not grand promises.

Consciousness grows daily.

No One Heals Alone

If you could heal alone, you already would have.

Every man needs:

- guidance
- books
- honest conversations
- therapy or mentorship
- healthy masculine role models

Healing is not an individual act.
It is a supported process.

Seeking help does not make you weak.
It makes you responsible.

Healing Changes the Way You Love

When a man heals:

- he stops reacting like a child
- he begins responding like an adult
- he stops controlling and starts trusting
- he stops running and starts staying
- he stops repeating patterns and starts choosing differently

Healing transforms relationships—not because others change,
but because *you* do.

What You Don't Heal, You Pass On

Children don't learn what you say.
They learn what you live.

There is no greater pain than passing on the same wounds that marked you.

Healing is not only personal.
It is generational.

The Final Truth

Healing is not easy.
But staying the same is far worse.

The pain of healing is temporary.
The pain of not healing becomes a lifetime.

If something moved inside you while reading this,
if you recognized yourself,
this chapter is your sign.

Stop running.
Stop justifying.
Stop hiding.

There is a strong, conscious, grounded man inside you.
Your wounds won't let you become him, unless you decide to heal.

And that decision… can begin today.

CHAPTER 49

The Courage to Look Within

The Most Masculine, Powerful, and Difficult Act a Man Can Do

A great number of men can lift weight.
They can work hard.
They can endure physical pain.
They can face the world every day.

But looking within or seeing themselves without defenses...
that is something very few dare to do.

Because external strength is simple.
Internal strength is another story.

It is emotional.
It is spiritual.
It is character.

It is the strength of the man who dares to see himself, truly, without a mask, without ego, and without excuses.

Looking Within Means Uncovering What You've Always Hidden

Every man carries an inner world he rarely acknowledges:

- wounds he never accepted
- fears he never voiced
- guilt he hid
- shame that marked him
- memories he avoids
- mistakes that still hurt
- emptiness he doesn't know how to fill

Looking inward requires confronting, with unwavering honesty, the truths you have sidestepped for years.

It means stopping the justifications.
Stopping the pretending.
Stopping the phrase, "That's just how I am."

It means seeing yourself as you are to become who you can be.

The Man Who Looks Within Stops Repeating Patterns

Some men live disconnected from the present:

They love the way they were hurt.
They yell the way they were yelled at.
They control the way they were controlled.
They avoid the way they were avoided.
They run the way they were abandoned.

And they don't do it out of malice.

But perhaps they should ask themselves:

- Why do I react this way?
- What fear controls me?
- What pattern am I repeating without realizing it?
- Does this come from my present… or from my childhood?
- Am I acting as a man… or as a wounded child?

When a man looks within, he changes his story.
When he doesn't, he repeats it.

Looking Within Is Not About Blaming Yourself, It's About Understanding Yourself

Some refuse to look at their pain because they believe it is weakness.

But it's the opposite:

Looking within doesn't accuse you.
Looking within explains you.

It explains why you love the way you do.
Why you fear the way you fear.
Why you react the way you react.

Why do commitment, trust, communication, or following through feel so hard.

Understanding yourself is the beginning of emotional freedom.

Courage Is Not What You Face Outside, but What You Face Inside

Being brave is not fighting, yelling, or enduring.

That's the easy part.

The hard part is saying:
"I am wounded."
"I am afraid."
"I don't know how to do this better."
"I need help."
"I want to change."

That kind of courage, emotional courage,
is what transforms an ordinary man into a great man.

Looking Within Makes You More Secure, Not Weaker

Men who refuse to look within live escaping:
They escape their emotions.
They escape deep conversations.
They escape responsibility.
They escape their own truth.

But when a man dares to see himself as he truly is,
he gains something that no gym, job, or external success can give him:

Inner security.

The woman by his side feels it.
His family feels it.
Life itself feels it.

A man who knows himself is a man who can be trusted.

Looking Within Is a Gift to You... and to Those You Love

When a man knows himself, he changes:

- he becomes more patient
- more conscious
- more loving
- more stable
- more reliable
- more present
- more human

And everything around him begins to flourish:
His relationship.
His home.
His energy.
His future.
His capacity to love.

Because no one forgets a man who chose to heal instead of repeat.

Looking Within Is the Beginning of a New Life

This chapter is an invitation.

A man who dares to look within also dares to change.
He dares to love better.
He dares to build himself.
He dares to become the best version he always suspected he could be.

Looking within is opening the door to a deeper, more conscious, and more dignified life.

Because the day you truly see yourself…
is the day you begin to truly *be*.

CHAPTER 50

Admiration: The Secret Language of Female Desire

It's not about being perfect, it's about being admirable.

There is a truth that almost no man knows, yet it silently determines the fate of a relationship:

A woman can only truly desire a man she admires.

It's not his face.
It's not his body.
It's not his money.
It's not his status.

It's his essence.

Admiration is the engine of female desire.
It's what makes her look at you with pride, with fire, with excitement.

When a woman admires her man, she respects him, follows him, chooses him, desires him… effortlessly.

Admiration is what awakens attraction, respect, emotional connection, and real desire.

It is the invisible fire that sustains what many men lose without understanding why.

Let me explain it to you:
when a woman stops admiring you...

She might still hold love for you, yet she no longer feels the same desire.

Because when admiration dies, everything dies with it.

And a man who is not admired becomes a companion,
but never an unforgettable man.

Admiration Is the "Charm" They Don't Understand

There are men born with emotional intelligence, charisma, inner strength, elegance, kindness, vision...

And even if they are not the most handsome, they inspire.

And a woman, in front of a man who inspires, melts.

But there are also men who, even if they are physically attractive,
have nothing inside that makes her admire them.

Not because they are bad men,
but because no one taught them that female attraction is born from who a man **IS**,
not from what he **APPEARS** to be.

And that, my friends... is sad and real.

What a Man Doesn't Know

A woman loses interest when she stops admiring him.

A woman can live with a man who is imperfect, broken, in process, growing...

but she cannot live with a man without an inner life.

Because admiration is born from seeing in him:

- vision
- curiosity
- emotional intelligence
- inner strength
- purpose
- self-leadership
- natural (or learned) charisma
- firm kindness
- constant growth
- initiative
- self-confidence without arrogance

A woman doesn't focus on the wallet (okay, maybe not all of them do).
Nor on the car.
Nor on the muscles.

A woman focuses on what he **EMITS**.

The Man Who Abandons His Essence... Loses Admiration

When a man stops growing, stops moving, stops learning, stops dreaming, stops having his own inner world…

A woman no longer looks up to admire him.

She looks to the side… and sees him just like everyone else.

He doesn't stand out.
He doesn't seduce.
He doesn't inspire.

A man without inner spark
not only stops inspiring her… he stops attracting her.

The Hard but NECESSARY Part

Men believe women lose desire because "something is missing sexually" …

NO.

What's missing is admiration.

Without admiration, female sexuality shuts down.

She needs to look at that man and think:
"What pride to walk beside him."
"What a mind."
"What presence."
"What energy."
"What a way of being."

If she doesn't think it… she disconnects.

This Is Not Genetics: It's Training

Here comes the liberating part:

There is no masculine skill that cannot be learned.

- Charisma can be trained
- Inner leadership can be built
- Emotional intelligence can be developed
- Communication can be learned
- Vision can be defined
- Purpose can be chosen
- Presence can be cultivated
- Confidence can be formed
- Emotional elegance can be practiced

It's not about being born charming.
It's about growing until you become a man worthy of admiration.

What They Must Know — and No One Tells Them

Female admiration is NOT bought.
NOT demanded.
NOT begged for.
NOT bragged about.

It is earned.

Every day.
Through actions.
Through coherence.
Through growth.
Through presence.
Through authenticity.

When a man builds himself…
she admires him without him having to ask.

When There Is No Admiration, the Relationship Empties

This is what men rarely understand:

When a woman stops admiring her partner, she feels:

- boredom
- disconnection
- lack of desire
- demotivation
- disinterest
- emotional loneliness
- lack of inspiration

It's not malice.
It's not ingratitude.
It's not a whim.

It's emotional biology.
It's feminine nature.

A woman cannot feel attracted to a man who stopped moving, growing, dreaming, or showing himself alive.

Routine kills desire.
But lack of admiration buries it.

The Final Truth

Admiration is the fuel of feminine love.
It is the bridge between emotional connection and physical desire.

It is what makes a relationship alive, deep, passionate, and real.

If you want a woman to love you, make her fall in love.
If you want her respect, show her character.
If you want her to follow you, show her direction.
If you want her to desire you, become an admirable man.

Because an admirable man is not built outside...
he is built within.

And when you do, you don't just earn her admiration...
you earn your own greatness.

CHAPTER 51

The Man His Children Respect

Your true legacy is not what you give them, but who you are in their eyes

Many men want their children to listen to them.
But few ask themselves whether they are truly men worth listening to.

Many fathers demand respect.
But almost none understand that respect is not demanded,
it is earned…
day by day, gesture by gesture, glance by glance.

This chapter is not here to judge you.
It is here to remind you of something immense:

You shape the idea your children will have about love, character, and life.
What they see in you, not what you say,
is what they will one day become or allow.

Your Children Don't Need a Superhero

They don't need the strongest man.
Nor the one with the most money.

Nor the one who never makes mistakes.
Nor the one who pretends to have all the answers.

They need you real.
Human.
Present.
Consistent.

Children don't respect perfection.
They respect honesty.
They respect the father who feels, takes responsibility, and builds with love.

They Learn More from Your Silences Than from Your Speeches

Your tone.
The way you look at them.
How you handle stress.
The way you treat their mother.
How you apologize.
How you face your mistakes.

All of that is tattooed into a child's emotional memory.

You can repeat a thousand times, "Respect your mother."
But if you humiliate her, ignore her, or treat her with indifference...
the REAL message is that.

Children copy what they see, not what they hear.

The Man His Children Respect Is Not Perfect He Is Responsible

Your children respect the man who:

- keeps his promises
- admits when he is wrong
- repairs what he breaks
- faces life without running away
- takes responsibility for his mistakes
- works for what he wants
- guides without yelling
- protects without dominating

Responsibility is the most mature form of love.

Respect Is Born from What They Feel When You Arrive

There are men whose presence brings:

- silence
- fear
- tension
- unease

And there are men whose arrival brings:

- peace
- laughter
- security
- trust

Ask yourself honestly:
Which version of you do your children recognize?

A True Father Teaches How to Love... by Loving Well

They learn from you:

- how to speak in a relationship
- how to resolve conflict
- how to apologize
- how to express affection
- how to protect without harming
- how to build a home

The way you treat their mother will quietly become
the measure of what they will one day tolerate or repeat.

Your Children Respect the Man Who Respects Himself

They respect the father who:

- grows
- improves
- learns
- heals
- takes care of himself
- sets boundaries
- walks away from what is toxic
- works on his character

A man who respects himself... teaches respect.

An Admirable Father Is One Who Builds, Not One Who Destroys

He builds with his words.
He builds with his example.
He builds with his decisions.
He builds with the way he loves.

Your children may forget a thousand details.
But they will never forget how they felt by your side.

That emotional imprint lasts a lifetime.

The Greatest Inheritance You Can Leave Them

It is not money.
Nor property.
Nor titles.
Nor businesses.

It is the peace of having had a good father:

- firm
- present
- noble
- stable
- responsible
- loving
- consistent

That is true generational wealth.

Being a Man, Respected by His Children Is an Honor That Is Built

It is built when you:

- listen to them
- understand them
- teach limits with love
- keep your word
- don't promise what you can't fulfill
- apologize without shame
- look at them with pride
- hug them without holding back

Your children don't need a perfect man... they need a committed one.

One who tries.
One who learns.

One who changes.
One who loves.

And that man, my friend...
that man will always earn the most sincere and deepest respect that exists.

CHAPTER 52

The Man You Yourself Desire to Be

When you stop living on autopilot and decide to build yourself with intention

Most men know perfectly well what kind of man they do **not** want to be… but very few have courageously asked themselves:

Who is the man **I** desire to become?

Not the one others expect.
Not the one your family shaped.
Not the one your pain constructed.
Not the one your ego invented to survive.

But *you*.
The real you.
The man you have not yet allowed yourself to be.

This chapter is an invitation to look at yourself
without fear, without masks, and without justifications.

The Man You Are Today... You Built Without Realizing It

You became a man the best way you could:
through life's blows, through culture, through necessity, through wounds, through example... or through the lack of it.

But almost never through conscious choice.

Perhaps you imitated your father,
or promised yourself you would never be like him.

Perhaps you learned to harden yourself so no one could break you.
Perhaps you learned to stay silent because no one listened to you.

But none of that defines who you can become.

Your past explains your behavior,
but it does not determine your destiny.

The Man You Desire to Be Lives Inside You

You feel him sometimes.
In your silences.
In your difficult nights.
In that discomfort that appears when you know you are not being your best version.

That man appears when you tell yourself:
"I know I can be better."

And not better for others.
Better for you.

More honest.
More present.
More stable.
More human.

That desire is not a whim:
it is your true identity knocking at the door.

That Man Already Has Shape, Even If You Can't Describe Him Yet

He is not perfect.
He is not invincible.
He is not a hero.

He is a man who:

- thinks before reacting
- feels without fearing weakness
- decides without impulses
- speaks with truth
- loves without harming
- is firm without being aggressive
- is strong without being arrogant
- is responsible without feeling imprisoned
- is free without being irresponsible

That man exists.
He is inside you.
He only needs you to shape him.

The Man You Desire to Be Is NOT Born... He Is Built

And he is built like this:

- **With awareness.**
  You stop living on autopilot and begin choosing how you speak, how you react, how you love.
- **With emotional discipline.**
  You understand that your character is worth more than your mood.
- **With humility.**
  You recognize that you must learn, that making mistakes does not diminish you, and that asking for forgiveness enlarges you.
- **With inner courage.**
  You dare to review your wounds, not to blame yourself, but to free yourself from them.
- **With responsibility toward yourself.**
  You stop waiting for life or someone else to rescue you. You take the helm.

That man does not appear all at once.
He is worked on.
He is shaped.
He is refined.

And one day… he begins to show.

The Man You Desire to Be Watches You Every Day

Every time you say something that doesn't align with your values… he feels it.
Every time you react as the man you swore you would never be… he reminds you.

It is not guilt.
It is calling.

An inner whisper that says:
"That's not who you are, you are capable of more than that."

The Man You Desire to Be Is Formed in Small Decisions

In how you speak.
In how you listen.
In how you treat the one you love.
In how you treat yourself.
In how you handle frustration.
In how you respond when you are angry.
In how you repair when you fail.

A great man is not formed on grand stages.
He is formed in the details.

Don't Wait for Life to Force You to Change

Some men wake up only when they lose everything:
their partner, their home, their respect, their health, their peace.

But you don't have to get there.

You can wake up now.
You can be that man today.

The man who grows.
Who rebuilds himself.
Who takes his life seriously.
Who leaves a mark.
Who inspires.
Who loves with responsibility.

The man you yourself admire.

And When You Become That Man... Your Entire Life Changes

Your relationships heal.
Your partner looks at you with pride.
Your children learn from you.
Your decisions improve.
Your peace grows stronger.
Your character matures.
Your self-worth rises.

Because when you change on the inside,
everything around you changes too.

The Man You Desire to Be Is Right There

He is not a distant dream.
He is not fantasy.
He is not impossible.

He is your best version.
The one you avoided out of fear…
and searched for by instinct.

You only need to make one decision:

Be him.
Build him.
Honor him.
Choose him.

And never betray yourself again.

CHAPTER 53

Your Transformation Starts Today

No excuses, no fear, no postponing your own life

There comes a moment in every man's life when he can no longer keep ignoring himself.
An exact point where excuses, blame, "this is just how I am," and "when I can" come to an end.

That moment is today.

Because nothing will change on the outside
until something changes on the inside.

This chapter is not here to comfort you.
It is here to wake you up.
To put a mirror in front of you.
To remind you that living halfway is also a way of dying.

A Man's Favorite Excuse: "I'll Start Tomorrow"

That "tomorrow" has stolen opportunities, relationships, respect, stability, and peace from you.
It has taken more from you than any person ever has.

The truth is simple:

If you don't start today, you won't start tomorrow.

Because it's not a lack of time.
It's not a lack of opportunities.
It's not a lack of resources.

It's a lack of decision.

Change Isn't What Scares You... Facing Yourself Is

Most men are not afraid of change.
They are afraid of admitting:

- "I can't keep going like this."
- "I am wounded."
- "I have hurt others."
- "I have habits that destroy me."
- "I have settled."
- "I don't like who I am becoming."

True courage is not about lifting weights,
it's about lifting your own truths.

And I want to tell you something powerful:

When you dare to look yourself straight in the face,
you discover the strength that was always there.

If You Want to Change, Stop Justifying Yourself

Men are not divided into strong or weak.
They are divided into those who justify themselves
and those who transform.

The man who justifies himself says:

- "That's just how I am."
- "Life made me this way."
- "She failed too."
- "I don't have time."
- "At this age, it's too late."
- "I'm explosive—what can I do?"
- "I'm just not affectionate."

That is not identity.
That is fear in disguise.

The man who changes says:

- "I need to improve."
- "I don't want to repeat my past."
- "I need to learn."
- "My wounds are controlling me, and I don't want that."
- "I want to be better than yesterday."

He is not perfect, but he is honest.
And honesty transforms.

Transformation Doesn't Start with Your Partner... It Starts with You

Many men only want to change when they are about to lose everything.
They change out of fear, not awareness.

But change driven by fear doesn't last.
Change driven by self-respect does.

If you don't respect yourself, no one else will.
If you don't value yourself, you won't know how to value others.
If you don't heal, you will destroy even what you love most.

Your partner is a mirror.
Your growth is reflection.

How Does Real Change Begin?

Not with giant goals.
Not with motivational speeches.
Not with empty promises.

It begins like this:

With an uncomfortable truth:
"There is something wrong in me, and I am going to face it."

With a firm decision:
"No more excuses, I start today."

With a small action, repeated daily:
a new habit, an honest conversation,
a respected boundary, a corrected behavior, a sincere apology,
an impulse you choose not to follow.

Transformation is not an event.
It is training.

Don't Punish Yourself... But Don't Lie to Yourself Either

Some men never change because they live in extremes:

A) They blame themselves so much that they believe they can no longer be better.
B) They justify themselves so much that they believe they don't need to be better.

Both routes lead to destruction.

The real balance is this:

Be compassionate with your past.
Be responsible for your future.

Because your childhood was not your fault,
but your adulthood *is* your responsibility.

Change Is Noticeable, Even If You Don't Talk About It

When a man begins to transform:

- his tone changes
- his patience improves
- his energy calms
- his character strengthens
- his way of loving matures
- his presence becomes secure
- his partner feels it
- his children admire him
- he begins to like himself

Not because he is perfect, but because he is consistent.

And a consistent man is a powerful man.

Today Is That Day

Not tomorrow.
Not when "you have time."
Not when life forces you.
Not when it's too late.

Today.

Today you decide whether to stay the same or grow.
Today you decide whether to react or learn to respond.
Today you decide whether to remain the man you were
or become the man you yourself would respect.

Today you decide to change your life...
before life changes it for you by force.

Don't do it for her.
Not for your children.
Not for the world.

Do it for you.

To sleep in peace.
To look at your reflection without shame.
To feel that you own yourself.
To stop living on excuses.
To become the man you always knew you could be.

So that one day, you can look at your life and say:

"I was brave.
I was honest.
I was a man."

CHAPTER 54

Simple Things That Make Women Fall in Love (And Men Have No Idea How Important They Are)

A real guide based on truths women live, remember... and never forget.

A man may have money, muscles, intelligence, or charm...
but nothing makes a woman fall in love like a detail thought out with intention.

Most men believe that making a woman fall in love is difficult.
The truth is, it's simple... if you know how to do it well.

This chapter is born from real stories—including some from my own life—not to show off, but to show what attentive love looks like...
and how any man, with or without money, can replicate that essence.

Thinking Before the Date (Instead of Improvising)

There is nothing more passion-killing than:

- "What do you want to eat?"
- "Where do you want to go?"

That's not attention.
That's emotional disorganization.

A man who plans says without words:
"I thought about you before seeing you."

Suggestion:
Choose two places and let her pick.
That's enough to make her feel cared for.

The Magic of Small, Consistent Details

Let me tell you the truth:

A woman never forgets the man who makes her feel chosen every day, not just at the beginning.

In my five-and-a-half-year relationship, there was something that marked my heart:
NEVER, not a single Friday, did he fail to send me a bouquet of roses.

Not flowers for birthdays.
Not flowers to apologize.
Flowers just because.

Flowers that said: "You are in my life, and I celebrate you."

And pay attention:
You don't need to send flowers every week.
What matters is consistency, not the price.

Details That Are Born from Listening

Once, I casually mentioned a book.
Nothing more.

Masculine Presence That Conquers Without Effort

A man captivates when he:

- notices what she needs
- anticipates without being asked
- listens with his heart
- gets ready to see her
- looks at her as if she were the only woman in the restaurant
- remembers what she said weeks ago

An attentive man becomes unforgettable, even if the relationship ends.

Because details make you fall in love…
but **PRESENCE** leaves a mark forever.

The Details Women Love (And Men Never Imagine)

- showing up showered and smelling good
- opening the car door
- walking on the street side of the sidewalk
- carrying her bag without complaining
- saying "Did you drink water today?"
- covering her when she falls asleep
- placing a hand on her back while walking
- sending flowers on an ordinary day
- remembering a date she forgot
- surprising her with her favorite snack
- arriving with a coffee "just because"

They are such simple things… yet so deeply feminine.

Chapter Closing

The men who make women fall in love are not the richest,
nor the most handsome,
nor the most popular.

They are the ones who think.
The ones who observe.
The ones who listen.
The ones who remember.
The ones who care.

You don't need an airplane to make a woman fall in love.
You need intention.
And consistency.
And attention.

CHAPTER 55

What Women Wish Men Truly Understood

A feminine perspective meant to guide, not to attack

This chapter is not written to criticize you.
It is written to help you see.

Because many men truly want to do things right…
they just don't always know how.

This is not about perfection.
It's about awareness.

There are small things, often invisible to men, that deeply affect attraction, connection, and emotional safety.
And when these things are ignored, relationships slowly fade, not because of lack of love, but because of lack of understanding.

Presence matters more than appearance

Personal presentation is not about vanity.
It's about respect, toward yourself and toward the woman you're with.

A man who takes care of himself communicates, without words:
"I value myself, and I value this moment."

Neglect, poor hygiene, or lack of effort, especially at the beginning, doesn't feel "authentic" to a woman.
It feels like disinterest.

Hygiene, punctuality, and personal care are not mere details; they are expressions of respect.

Conversation is emotional foreplay

Many women don't disconnect because a man is not attractive.
They disconnect because he has no inner world.

Repeating the same topics, having nothing to say, or showing no curiosity about life slowly kills attraction.
A man with dreams, ideas, questions, and direction is magnetic.

It's not about impressing.
It's about being alive inside.

An interesting man doesn't talk about everything... But he has something to say.

Direction is attractive

A man doesn't need to have everything figured out.
But a man who doesn't know where he's going, or who shows no intention of moving, creates emotional insecurity.

Passion, purpose, and goals don't just build a future.
They build desire.

Money does not replace intention

Not all women are impressed by money.
Most are moved by thoughtfulness.

Small gestures, consistency, attention, and effort often mean more than expensive dinners or gifts.
Luxury fades.
Intention stays.

Control kills attraction

Wanting to know everything, monitoring, questioning excessively, or disguising control as "care" slowly suffocates love.

A woman does not feel protected by control.
She feels diminished by it.

Trust fosters intimacy.
Control undermines it.

True security is not shown through domination, but rather by finding peace within yourself.

Routine requires creativity

Routine without intention becomes emotional neglect.

Women don't need constant excitement.
They need presence, creativity, and the feeling that the relationship is still being chosen, not just maintained.

Laziness is not masculinity

A man who avoids responsibility, initiative, or effort feels more like a burden than a partner.

No woman wants to feel like she's raising an adult child.
Partnership requires movement.

Desire is emotional, not mechanical

Sex is not just physical for women.

When intimacy is treated as a biological function instead of an emotional exchange, something essential breaks.

True desire is unlocked through effective communication, emotional safety, and being fully present.

Fidelity is not optional

Infidelity destroys something that cannot fully be repaired.

Even when forgiveness happens, something inside the woman changes forever.

Respect, loyalty, and integrity are not romantic ideals.
They are emotional necessities.

Criticism is not always an attack

When a woman offers feedback, it's often because she cares, not because she wants to control you or change who you are.

Listening without defensiveness is one of the most mature masculine skills.

Vulnerability is attractive

Women are not repelled by male emotions.

They are repelled by emotional absence.

A man who can feel, express, cry, and be honest builds intimacy, not weakness.

Don't rush intimacy. Genuine interest does not invade, it builds.

Genuine interest fosters connection rather than imposing it.

Building intimacy is about patience and presence, allowing trust to grow naturally over time. When you honor her boundaries and listen deeply, you show her that you value her as a person, not just as a partner.

Don't promise what you can't sustain. Coherence makes you fall in love more than intensity.

Consistency builds trust far more than grand gestures or fleeting passion.

Stay committed to your promises and ensure your actions align with your intentions, even when things feel uncertain or slow. Remember, intimacy thrives when you respect her boundaries and approach her with patience, presence, and a willingness to listen attentively. It's in these quiet moments of genuine care that lasting connection is built.

Final reflection

This chapter is not about blame.
It's about clarity.

Many relationships don't fail because love disappears.
They fail because awareness never arrives.

If you read this with an open heart, not a defensive one, you will not feel attacked.
You will feel guided.

Because the man who listens, grows.
And the man who grows... becomes unforgettable.

FINAL CHAPTER

A Message for the Man Who Wants to Do Things Right

The ending you didn't expect... but the one you needed to read.

I don't know who you are.
I don't know your story.
I don't know your pain, your fears, or your defeats.
I don't know what you did, what you avoided, or what you're trying to repair.

But if you made it this far,
truly this far,
that means something enormous:

You want to do things right.

And that desire alone already places you in a different place than many men.

Because men who destroy don't read.
Those who run don't look at themselves.
Those who don't feel don't search for answers.
And those who don't care... never reach a final chapter like this.

But you did.

And that already says who you can become.

You Were Not Born Knowing How to Be a Man

This needs to be clear:

Not everyone was taught how to manage emotions.
Not everyone was shown how to love.
Not everyone grew up seeing examples of responsibility, respect, self-control, and emotional presence.

Many became men the only way they could:
through blows, through silence, through lack, through repetition, through survival.

Sometimes you imitated what you hated.
Sometimes you repeated what you swore you would never do.
And sometimes you simply didn't know how to do better.

That's not an excuse.
It's the truth.

But today, here, now,
you no longer have an excuse not to change.

Your Past Explains... But It Does Not Justify

You may have lived a hard childhood.
A confusing adolescence.
A life marked by wounds.

All of that explains how you react.
But it does **not** justify how you treat others.

You were hurt, yes.
But that does not authorize you to hurt.

You suffered, yes.
But that does not give you permission to cause suffering.

The past is the starting point.
Not the destination.

Being a Good Man Is Not About Being Perfect: It's About Being Responsible

Women are not looking for perfection.
They are looking for coherence.

They are not looking for heroes.
They are looking for presence.

They are not looking for muscles.
They are looking for self-control.

They are not looking for speeches.
They are looking for actions.

And you can be that man.
You truly can.

You don't need fame.
You don't need to be a millionaire.
You don't need to be the most handsome or the strongest.

You only need courage:
the courage to recognize, to grow, to ask for help, to correct, to try again.

Love Doesn't Transform You... What You Do for Love Does

Loving is not about feeling good.
It's about choosing well.

Choosing to speak when you want to shout.
Choosing to stay when you want to run.
Choosing to understand when you want to fight.
Choosing to respect when you could impose yourself.
Choosing to build when your ego wants to destroy.

Love is not proven through passion.
It is proven through consistency.

If You Want to Be a Man Worth Having, Start Here

A short list,
but one capable of changing everything:

- **Ask for forgiveness without excuses.**
  Excuses kill forgiveness.
- **Speak clearly.**
  No one reads minds. You don't either.
- **Keep your word.**
  Your word is your reputation.
- **Listen without defending yourself.**
  Maturity begins when you don't need to win.
- **Control your impulses.**
  No one respects a man who doesn't govern himself.
- **Work on yourself.**
  What you don't heal, you repeat.
- **Don't hurt those who love you.**
  Even if you have reasons... you don't have the right.

- **Learn to lose.**
  Sometimes you win by letting go.
- **Be protective without controlling.**
  Strength is not violence. Care is not possession.
- **Become the man YOU yourself would respect.**
  That is true success.

The Most Important Truth: You Still Can

It doesn't matter what you did.
It doesn't matter how many times you failed.
It doesn't matter who stopped believing in you.

As long as you breathe, you can be better.
As long as you have awareness, you can correct.
As long as you have pain, you can transform.
As long as you have love, even if it's only your own, you can rebuild yourself.

It's never too late to be the man you should have been.
It's never too late to be the man you want to be.
It's never too late to be the man someone deserves.

But above all:
it's never too late to be the man **YOU** admire.

If You're Here... It's Because You've Already Started to Change

This book does not judge you.
It guides you.
It shows you.
It confronts you.
It shakes you.
It wakes you up.

But above all:
this book opens the possibility for you to become the man you always wanted to be...
but never knew where to begin.

And if you made it to this point,
it's because you already took the first step.

FINAL NOTE FROM THE AUTHOR

If there is one thing I want you to remember from this book, it is this:
It doesn't matter where you come from.
What matters is where you choose to go.
It doesn't matter what you did.
What matters is what you choose to do now.
It doesn't matter who failed you.
What matters is who you choose to become.

Being a man is not a burden.
It is not a performance.
It is not a pose.
It is not a shield.

Being a man is a path.
And like any path, it is walked step by step:
with humility, intention, responsibility, respect,
and a heart willing to evolve.

You are more capable than you think.
More valuable than you were told.
And stronger than you imagine.

This book ends here... but your story does not.
What you do after closing these pages
will be your true final chapter.

I hope you write one you can be proud of.

Thank you for making it this far.
Thank you for choosing yourself.
Thank you for wanting to do things right.

ABOUT THE AUTHOR

Olivia Lambragno is a writer, mentor, and creator of reflective works focused on emotional growth, conscious relationships, and personal transformation.

Through her writing, Olivia explores the inner world of men and women with honesty, depth, and compassion. Her work addresses themes such as emotional responsibility, healing, self-awareness, love, and personal evolution, always from a place of truth rather than judgment.

Her approach is direct yet deeply empathetic. She invites readers to look within, take responsibility for their choices, and build a life aligned with who they truly want to become, not who they were taught to be.

Olivia believes that transformation does not begin with perfection, but with awareness, courage, and consistency. Her work is rooted in real experiences and emotional truth, guided by the conviction that growth is possible at any stage of life.

This book was written for those who want to do better, not to be flawless, but to be conscious, present, and responsible. It is an invitation to grow, heal, and become someone you can respect and feel proud of.

Olivia writes to awaken, to guide, and to remind readers that their past does not define them… their choices do.

You can learn more about Olivia's work at:

www.olivialambragno.com

Made in the USA
Coppell, TX
25 March 2026

74624828R00184